HOME ECONOMICS
and
FEMINISM

The
Hestian Synthesis

HOME ECONOMICS
and
FEMINISM

The
Hestian Synthesis

Patricia J. Thompson

Home Economics Publishing Collective
UPEI
1988

Distribution by the
Department of Home Economics
University of Prince Edward Island
Charlottetown, P.E.I.
C1A 4P3

Published by the
Home Economics Publishing Collective, UPEI

Irene Burge   Jean MacKay
Heather Gillis   Estelle Reddin
Heather Henry   Nancy Reddin

Production & Design: Ken Shelton
Illustration: P. John Burden
Typesetting: Braemer Publishing
Printing: Les Éditions Marquis

ACKNOWLEDGEMENTS

The Publishing Collective acknowledges the contribution of the participants of the workshop "Home Economics and Feminism: The Hestian Synthesis" held prior to the 1986 Canadian Home Economics Association Conference in Charlottetown. During the workshop at Belcourt Centre, Sister Bernice Cullen graciously attended to the comfort and well-being of the participants.

The Collective expresses thanks to Janie Saunders for the preparation of the text, to Vicki Reddin Gauthier for proof reading, and to Barbara Curley for assistance with transcribing records of the proceedings.

We greatly appreciate the support of the University of Prince Edward Island, the Prince Edward Island Home Economics Association, the Canadian Home Economics Association, and The Women's Programme, Secretary of State. The members of the Collective appreciate receiving permission from *Common Ground* to reproduce, "The Stereotype Sisters," and from Dramatists Play Service, Inc. for excerpts from *Quilters*.

WORKSHOP PARTICIPANTS

Carmen Babineau
Centre universitaire de Moncton
Moncton, N.B.

Irene Burge
U.P.E.I.
Charlottetown, P.E.I.

Joan M. Casey
Education Consultant
St. John's, Newfoundland

Marcelle Dugas
Centre universitaire de Moncton
Moncton, N.B.

Linda Eyre
Teacher
Wolfville, N.S.

Elizabeth Feniak
University of Manitoba
Winnipeg, Manitoba

Beverley Gardner
Teacher
St. John's, Newfoundland

Heather Gillis
Student, U.P.E.I.
Charlottetown, P.E.I.

Betty Gordon
Teacher
Bronx, N.Y.

Heather Henry
U.P.E.I.
Charlottetown, P.E.I.

Aline Landry
Conseillère en sciences familiales
Fredericton, N.B.

Lynda G. MacCulloch
Acadia University
Wolfville, N.S.

Jean MacKay
U.P.E.I.
Charlottetown, P.E.I.

Lorraine MacLeod
Home Economics Coordinator
Moncton, N.B.

Gaye Meredith Mullins
Graduate Student
Pointe Claire, P.Q.

Heather Oxford
Advisory Council on the
Status of Women
Charlottetown, P.E.I.

J. Estelle Reddin
U.P.E.I.
Charlottetown, P.E.I.

Nancy Reddin
Home Economist
Montague, P.E.I.

Tanya Trembley
Curriculum Consultant
Fredericton, N.B.

Wanda Young
University of Saskatchewan
Saskatoon, Saskatchewan

To the memory of Dr. Beatrice Paolucci
scholar, mentor, friend

PREFACE

As President I am indeed happy to write a brief preface to this publication, for what was said and argued by the conference leader, Patricia J. Thompson, is a strong affirmation of the rightful place of Home Economics among the disciplines appropriate for a small undergraduate university dedicated to upholding the traditions of the liberal arts.

But I have a second reason for my pleasure. As a Classicist I am intrigued by the proposed use of those ancient Greek gods Hestia and Hermes as symbols of two contrasting worlds. The guardian of the hearth, Hestia, is thought to represent that invisible world that is centered around the home. Hermes, as patron of the marketplace, becomes a statement of that highly visible world of politics or, as the Greeks would say, of those things that citizens do. I am prepared to believe that there is some value in using these symbols to summarize two quite different sets of actions and attitudes, sets that should be partners or at least complements, but not strangers.

Yet in other ways I hesitate to accept these new associations for Hestia and Hermes. The goddess was not only at the centre of each home; she was also at the centre of the city. In a way she proclaims a unity in the state: wherever there is a *polis*, there too is an *oikos*. As for Hermes, he had many roles. He was patron of commerce, thus his place in the market. He was something of a thief. And he played messenger. I find it hard to take him as seriously as a contrast with Hestia would suggest. And yet he did lead Persephone from Hades to Demeter on earth, daughter and mother together for part of the year. A Hestian relationship served by Hermes?

I am very grateful to the editors for introducing me to this conference and its challenging subject. By all means let us give Hestia and Hermes new life and meaning. But let us also remember that there was a time when both gods lived on Olympus, members of a large squabbling family, in which politics was played in front of the fire.

C.W.J. Eliot, President
University of Prince Edward Island
Charlottetown, P.E.I.
26 April 1987

IX

BELCOURT
CENTRE

FOREWORD

In the fall of 1984, I read in *What's New in Home Economics* an article so relevant to some of our professional concerns that I wrote to the author to tell her how strongly I agreed with her. Although I was not then acquainted with Dr. Patricia J. Thompson, my letters and her responses began a professional association and friendship that led to the pre-conference workshop on which this book is based.

From the outset I was impressed with Pat Thompson's provocative, enthusiastic, and optimistic approach to the problems of our discipline. I was amazed to find, as she tells us in the opening chapter of this volume, that she had explored a number of fields of study and work before "coming upon" Home Economics. Like America to Columbus, Home Economics was there all the time, awaiting her discovery! She came to the discipline as a mature and experienced person seeing with "new eyes", compared with those of us who travelled the usual route of undergraduate and graduate study. To my delight, I learned that she had been strongly influenced by an intellectual leader in our discipline, my dear friend the late Beatrice Paolucci under whom I was privileged to study for both the Master's and Doctor's degrees. Many home economists know her pioneering work on the family as an ecosystem and her many other contributions to theory and philosophy in Home Economics.

Pat shared with me copies of some of her talks, published articles, and work still in draft form. In these she introduced a metaphor from Greek mythology drawn from the goddess of the hearth, Hestia. This metaphor seems a useful symbol to explain who we are and what we stand for. The Hestian metaphor is intended to help home economists make essential linkages with feminist theory and the new women's scholarship. It will help us to communicate both within the profession and between home economists and outsiders.

When the Home Economics Department at the University of Prince Edward Island considered mounting a workshop prior to the 1986 Canadian Home Economics Association Convention in Charlottetown, the faculty decided it would be worthwhile and stimulating to explore further some of Pat Thompson's ideas—if we could persuade her to come. She could come. She did come. And she gave three days of strong leadership to the pre-conference workshop "Home Economics and Feminism: the Hestian Synthesis."

Belcourt Centre, at South Rustico, was an ideal locale for our meeting. A former convent and boarding school, it is comfortable but not luxurious. Overlooking the Gulf of St. Lawrence, this peaceful and beautiful spot, with its fresh, green farmlands, rich, red soil, sparkling blue waters, sunshine and fresh air is far from such city distractions as shopping malls and traffic. It provided an unhurried atmosphere wherein participants could concentrate, reflect, and interact. Sister Bernice Cullen, a retired professor from the University of Prince Edward Island, administers the Centre as a Retreat House. She was a gracious and generous hostess to the conference participants.

In bringing greetings from the University of Prince Edward Island, Dr. Lawson Drake, Dean of Science, described this atmosphere:

> I cannot guess how your discussions will go, but if, as I do, you place any value on Spirit of Place, I think you have an ideal location for your workshop in this Centre, which embodies traditions of innovation, contemplation, reflection and service, linking thought to action in many spheres of human relations.

His words were to prove prophetic. As the meetings progressed, participants relaxed and discussion and dialogue developed: private discussions at meals, nutrition breaks, and in shared living space added to the total experience. Printed Proceedings seemed an appropriate outcome. However, after we reread the transcribed tapes of the public meetings, a book seemed a better way to capture the gist and spirit of the meeting.

Two specially planned events contributed to the collective consciousness of the participants. The first, billed as a "divertissement," created a change of pace from serious discussion. A series of colored slides of handmade quilts that had been displayed in exhibits at the Confederation Centre of the Arts in Charlottetown was presented together with taped songs and dramatic readings from the musical play *Quilters*. The "divertissement" promoted poignant reflections on women's everyday lives.

The second event, which closed the workshop, was a buffet luncheon at my home, with the Spirit of Place once again linking us together.

Perhaps Dean Drake had some sense of the outcome of the workshop when he said:

> It would be presumptuous of me to attempt to lecture you on the diversity of Home Economics today. It is sufficient that I tell you that I am aware of that diversity and that I am most appreciative of any efforts which seek to express the unity of purpose which underlies the broad range of activities which typify Home Economics.

Ten Lake Placid Conferences (1899–1909) gave birth to the Home Economics profession. Dare we entertain the conceit that this 1986 workshop will prove to be another "Lake Placid Conference"? Might it bring about a whole new way of thinking and talking, about and within this profession in which many believe so strongly? Pat speaks of the "Hestian Imperative" and, towards the end of the meetings, speaks also of "empowering our Hestian profession." She challenges home economists to become Hestian feminists.

Is Prince Edward Island too small or remote a place from which to launch the concept of Hestian feminism? Precedents have already been established through events which occurred earlier in Prince Edward Island history. One was the agreement in 1864 to form Canada as a nation. Another was the publication of L.M. Montgomery's *Anne of Green Gables* which has travelled the world in its original form, as a long-running musical, and as a CBC-TV special. Ideas that have influenced Western thought and action throughout centuries spread outward from small islands in the Aegean. Perhaps Prince Edward Island is an apt place from which to desseminate the Hestian idea!

For us, this book captures the intellectual essence and the spirit of inquiry and interaction that developed during our days together. We hope it proves helpful to those wishing to carry this idea forward. We believe it provides an eye-opening and mind-expanding introduction to contemporary Home Economics for those concerned about the effects of patriarchy and the male/female gender dichotomy on personal and family life in today's society.

Jean Halliday MacKay, Ph.D.
Workshop Coordinator
Stanley Bridge, P.E.I.
Spring, 1987

CONTENTS

HOME ECONOMICS
and
FEMINISM

The
Hestian Synthesis

INTRODUCTION

AUTHENTICITY VS AUTHORITY: A PERSONAL VIEW

If analogy is not a method of demonstration in the true sense of the word, it is nevertheless a method of illustration and of secondary verification which may be of some use . . . . In fact, analogy is a legitimate form of comparison, and comparison is the only practical means we have for the understanding of things.

Emil Durkheim,
Sociology and Philosophy.

WHEN I LOOK back to the time when I wasn't in Home Economics (before I was editor for Home Economics texts), it seems incredible to me that such a transformation could take place in one human being. I'm a New Yorker. As a little girl I lived in the prairie province of Saskatchewan during terrible times, during the 1930s drought. My grandparents had a farm, and I went to a one-room schoolhouse in Parry, a tiny village in Saskatchewan. My maternal grandparents and great grandparents were farmers who owned large estates in Russia. My mother's family left Russia after the Revolution, settled in Canada, and some went to the States. It's difficult for urban people to understand the importance of things close to nature—the ecology of our wherewithal: food, clothing, fibre, shelter, wood—our basic resources. As a city person, I'm lucky to have had roots in rural areas. I have an ecological perspective engrained in my thinking.

Deprivation was an important component in my childhood. To be poor was important. I tell those who write rhetoric about poverty that I don't advocate poverty. I don't want people to be poor! But in looking back on the years of privation, I learned first-hand about ecology and resourcefulness. It was tough in Canada in the mid 30s, in Saskatchewan in the drought. My grandfather, who struggled very hard, died at that time. Since then, my uncles have done well. But the duality of the

1

urban person who has rural roots and knows what a fragile web the ecology is, how human life is caught up in natural events, has remained with me into my mature years.

I went to a New York City school for the gifted (I hoped to become a fine artist). It was a special high school for music and art majors. I majored in Fine Arts and thought I'd become a painter. Next I went to Barnard College where there was no Home Economics program. Barnard was then the women's college of Columbia University. I first majored in English. After I got 30 credits in English, I thought I'd be a lawyer. I took credits in Government. Then I went on to graduate school in Political Science, in International Law. I never seemed to fit anywhere! There was a little bit of Political Science that I liked, and a bit of English that I liked, and there was something about Anthropology that I liked, and there was something about Psychology that I liked. But I liked only parts of each. I never was fully brought into any field. I was a generalist with no discipline to call "home." When you're a generalist like that, what career is better than to become an editor—a magazine editor and a magazine writer? That's what I did.

Of all the kinds of magazines that I should fall heir to, I went into science fiction editing! In that job I tried to think of what the human condition would be, given rapid scientific changes. How would technological changes in our lifestyle affect people? One day in the 1950s I called General Foods and asked if they were doing any research on space food. The home economist at General Foods thought I was crazy. She told me they were not then doing research on space. But I began to wonder what everyday life would be like on another planet. What would it be like in a totally different environment? How would people meet their needs? And I wrote magazine columns about technology. I also wrote columns about romance, marriage, childbirth, and all kinds of "woman" things.

Later in life, after I had married and had a family, I got an opportunity to edit a Home Economics textbook. That was the beginning of a real change for me. My first response to Home Economics was, "What a piece of cake!" What an easy job! I had been editing Social Studies textbooks. And I asked myself, why not edit something where men aren't going to compete with me? Being a woman in business had certain disadvantages. I thought perhaps if I got into Home Economics editing, I would escape the competition, because men wouldn't want that job. In retrospect, I was being "set up" to become a feminist! I took the job of Home Economics editor thinking I could do it off the top of my head. Something strange happened. I found this puzzle, this mental puzzle, was challenging! It wasn't just getting food copy, clothing copy, housing copy, child development copy and family relationships copy. It all had to fit together. That was different. I could look at the text as a sociologist. There's the sociology of family, the sociology of food, and the sociology of clothing. There's also the sociology of shelter. And then I thought—there's psychology, the psychology of human development, child development, and family relationships and the psychology of housing and clothing. I found pieces that had to be brought together. There was food and nutrition, so in addition to Sociology and Psychology we would have to deal with the biological sciences. Then I realized that we had to deal with the science of genetics, not only in terms of foods and plants but in terms of people. And there was a science and a chemistry of fiber. There was also a history to these things. What was happening to my mind? I couldn't understand! There was something perplexing occurring intellectually. I had begun to see I would have to connect all these threads—Sociology, Psychology, History and the sciences—in one textbook! What a challenge it became. It has absorbed me ever since.

You in Home Economics had this already done for you. I had to go at it the hard way. Alone. I had to discover for myself that the chemistry of food and the chemistry of textiles were related to the chemistry of the environment. Ecology was not yet an idea whose time was about to come—again! Most important, human beings were being impacted by chemical and technological changes in the environment. So, as I worked on Home Economics texts in New York, some of my early point of view as a child in a farming community in Canada came back to remind me that everything was connected, that everything really could not be fragmented. To bring these assorted pieces of information into some integrated, comprehensive, vision of human life was a new kind of intellectual demand for me. It wasn't enough to do as I had done, which was "shop" the disciplines to get a little piece of knowledge here and a little piece of knowledge there. I didn't fully understand what was at work within me saying that this piece is relevant, that piece is not relevant. The relevant parts seemed to fit into a new pattern that I had begun to discern. It was Home Economics I saw! Home Economics provided a different intellectual pattern from the disciplines with which I was familiar. There was a uniqueness about it in terms of the connection of one piece of information to another. It was about relationships—of people, things, and ideas. It wasn't so obvious at first. It's embarrassing to admit that I thought Home Economics was a simple field to master. I was patronizing and condescending when I first encountered Home Economics: I thought other disciplines were superior. Fortunately, I changed. Why? Because I was curious. I had to find out the reason for this cognitive dissonance.

I was not fortunate enough to have had the perspective provided by a Home Economics education to help me. No one told me that there was a single field of study that had already solved some of these intellectual problems and that I could build on what Home Economics had already begun.

I began to examine epistemological problems as a textbook editor and writer. I went back to school and earned my first degree in Home Economics. I already had a Master's degree in the teaching of Social Studies. I had abandoned the International Law piece because I couldn't see myself as an international lawyer. I had a little son, and I found that I was very poorly equipped to be a mother. The courses that I had taken in college did not equip me to understand my child's development. Nothing that I had learned had prepared me to be a good parent or to live in a dual career marriage. Many things were excluded from my vision by my education, not by my family or my mother, but by the fact that I received an education that said that none of that was important. The education I had received was modelled upon the elitist education of patriarchal colleges designed for men. It took years for me to understand that I had been systematically excluded from education of central importance to my life as a female human being.

So I was stumbling along, looking for answers. The most astonishing thing was that I stumbled into Home Economics through this route of editing and publishing! Luckily, I found people patient enough to answer some of my naive questions. When you come to Home Economics as an outsider, it seems like alien territory. It is unfamiliar. You notice that the paradigms, the models of the disciplines that you're accustomed to, don't hold for Home Economics. And when you're trained as I was, the first thing you think is that there is something wrong with Home Economics! Now if Home Economics would just shape up, I thought, and change its name, improve its image, all this would change. That was my attitude. Name change was imperative! Becoming more "scientific" was essential. We could do away with some of the less important parts of Home Economics. I had the frame of reference that came out of an "elitist" education. The home economists with whom I dealt were sufficiently committed to help me. I was working with Dora S. Lewis, past-president of the American Home Economics Association, editing her high school textbooks. She was patient. As I put this intellectual mosaic together, she helped me to see how pieces of information from different disciplines could be integrated and make sense as a comprehensive study of everyday life. Later, Beatrice Paolucci made me aware of the intellectual challenge Home Economics represented.

I began to change. From one who was an advocate for name change for Home Economics, I studied the history and philosophy of the field. It's easy for people such as I was to find fault with Home Economics. It is dangerous when people like I was become Home Economics supervisors and administrators in Home Economics units. They have the point of view I once had. They do not see that Home Economics represents a different point of view. Because I was trained in the social sciences, I went into the history of the field. I read the entire collection of the Proceedings of the Lake Placid Conferences. I read the entire collection of American and Canadian Home Economics journals from the beginning up until 1983, which was the last time I had a chance to do that. I read everything I could about Home Economics.

I began to understand what Sarah Arnold, the Dean of Simmons College in the 1900s, meant when she said, "We have come upon an altogether new discipline." And that is what I believe Home Economics is: an altogether new discipline, a discipline unlike any discipline that existed before and unlike any other discipline that exists now. But it is a discipline that is often hard to articulate, because there are many people whose point of view on Home Economics is like mine used to be.

Why do people have this stance toward Home Economics? Why is it that when one tries to explain Home Economics, somebody will say, "See you later. I already know. I grew up in a family. I eat three meals a day. I've got children. I know what Home Economics is!"

A Discipline of Everyday Life

Home Economics uses everyday language, vernacular language. It deals with events that are "commonplace." That is why it is perceived as commonplace, mundane, insignificant, and something that could well be taken care of in a "catch as catch can" way—a little piece of knowledge here, a little piece of knowledge there. But then it would be broken down to where I was when I began, that is, I had a little piece of Sociology, a little piece of Law, a little piece of Psychology, a little piece of Art, a little piece of Architecture, a little piece of Science. It didn't work for me as a female human being in a complex society. And I don't think it works for others, either. Each of us must create our life phenomenologically, from where we stand to where we're going. And we must weave together the knowledge that we have cognitively, as well as our unique affective responses to our experience and our environment. Nobody talks about those things. They are supposed to just happen—somehow. They are supposed to take care of themselves.

The question that I asked was why this negative feeling about Home Economics existed. For example: If you travel and somebody asks you what you do and you say, "I'm an astrophysicist," this person's whole behavior toward you becomes kind of awe-struck. But if you say "I'm a home economist," the person assumes he/she knows what you do, or they know what your interest is, or they know the limitations of your intelligence. They don't treat you the same way. What kind of a society is it in which if you are an astrophysicist you are terrific, but if you're a home economist, you're not so terrific? And the question seemed to me to require some full comprehension of what the discipline was about. Can a fish describe water? It's hard to ask home economists to describe what they do! We have this whole movement toward defining Home Economics, and it's very difficult for people who have always been home economists, who have never been outside the field, who have never perceived the field as negatively as I once did, to understand what the forces are around the discipline that make it hard for it to be taken seriously. Even to survive. So I asked the question: Why is Home Economics so negatively perceived? I believe it's gender! Most home economists are women. Therefore, I've turned to the feminist literature to ask, "What are the disadvantages of the female gender?" I went to college with some of the leaders of the feminist movement in the States, and I might tell you that they think I am a lapsed liberal to have become a home economist. They feel I'm a traitor to women's issues because I insist that Home Economics has most of the answers for the current feminist dilemma about women and families.

A great many women, a lot of young women today, do not feel drawn to what is called the "women's liberation movement." I take issue with the word "liberation" because none of us can be liberated from our connection to the biosphere. Human beings are irrevocably and irrefutably connected to the ecosystem of which they are part. There is no liberation from being human and meeting human needs. The question of why Home Economics has been so negatively perceived and why it is so difficult for home economists to communicate about Home Economics has occupied me for the past decade. I'm trying to work out some resolutions to the critical juncture that Home Economics appears to be in worldwide. It's not just in the States and in Canada: I think that there are problems worldwide, and I think that the so-called "women's liberation movement" has played a role in this.

For twenty years some in the women's movement have said that the family is a source of women's oppression. That's a fundamental tenet of some feminists—that the family is the reason women are disadvantaged. I don't accept that, because family still remains for me the most important social unit, and women have a unique relation to the family and they always have had. So I've undertaken something no less ambitious than to attack the whole edifice of patriarchal culture! My view is that the history of Western culture related to women and the family has been rendered invisible by forces over which women have had no control. We in Home Economics are disadvantaged by that invisibility. Women are invisible. Their role in society has been invisible. Their family contributions have not been counted in the gross national product of either of our countries. For that reason, much of what women have contributed through their work in families has been rendered invisible. That invisibility stems from an early decision in Western culture that only the public world has both visibility and value.

From Separate Spheres to Systems in Interaction

In the feminist literature a number of dichotomies are identified, and they play off each other. The French feminists have been very good at attacking dichotomies. Pairs that come to mind in terms of women's role in society are worthwhile/worthless, isolated/connected. Historically we have tended to dichotomize. The first dichotomy was the male/female gender dichotomy. A lot of attributes and characteristics flow from the gender factor. Feminists are hooked on discussion of gender roles. They have given much thought to the question of "difference." Home economists also need to talk about male/female, public/private, visible/invisible. Feminists have spoken of "separate spheres" as a negative thing.

I propose that there are two domains of human action, each characterized by a unique purpose. We could go on forever dichotomizing and end up with two piles that would be hard to sort out. I am approaching "twoness" somewhat differently by identifying two domains or systems of human action. One is the domain of human necessity. It came first. It is primal. It's the domain of everyday life in which people meet the need for food, for shelter, for clothing, for human connectedness, and for human development over the life course. It is a personal, private domain. It is characterized by care and connection. This domain contrasts with the domain of public action in which behaviour is dominated by group processes in the public sphere. Public life is characterized by hierarchy and control. You can look at two general spheres, or two gendered domains, or two systems of human action. One domain is private and invisible. It is absolutely essential for individual and species survival. The other domain is public and visible. Its activities are secondary to survival, and its primary purpose is to control people and resources. We create institutions for each of these domains to achieve these purposes. Both domains are grounded in the biosphere or physical, natural world in which all of us (for better or for worse) are embedded. There's not much we can do about that! However, we can do something about how we think about these dual domains—the private and the public.

Gender-intensive Is Not Gender-exclusive

We have to accept the fact that the human species has two "sexes." We create the two "spheres." Let's break away from the simplistic view of gendered human life. It seems short-sighted to perpetuate the notion of two gender-exclusive spheres. We know that men and women live in a private world. Both men and women occupy themselves with private, personal activities that become invisible. Both men and women occupy themselves with biologically and psychologically essential activities. And similarly, both men and women have become involved in public, visible, and surplus activities for their mutual support. So the two spheres are not gender-exclusive, but they have become gender-intensive. There are more women in the private sphere and more men in the public sphere. But whether or not they like to admit it, they enter and influence one another's domains! Thus a notion of systems in interaction seems more descriptive of the world we inhabit than the notion of separate spheres as isolated domains with no interaction between them. Let's think about these dual domains of human action as two systems in interaction. There can be outputs from one domain, inputs to and feedback from another domain. These two domains form dynamic interrelationships in the life of everyday human beings as they pursue their essential capacity to live as people and as members of families. Each domain has a characteristic institution. What would this be? The private domain has the family, and the public domain has the state.

The dichotomy that underlies the Western intellectual tradition goes back to classical times. I believe it accounts for the perpetuation of an elitist bias that can no longer be accepted uncritically.

Oikos and Polis: The Two Domains

The earliest descriptor of the domain of everyday necessity was the Greek *oikos* or household. Home Economics has always dealt with the household. The household is a temporal, fluid, spatial domain, organized to meet the essential demands of everyday life. The family is the institution that occupies the household. When communities were small and human groups were interdependent (i.e. the human group was one big family), everything was within the control of the oikos. In about the 4th century B.C., what institution developed? It was the *polis*, the city state. That paradigm persists in modern intellectual life. We accept that only the work of the polis, only the public sphere, only the visible activities "outside" everyday essential need have value. The sphere of everyday necessity—the oikos—has been devalued. We're dealing with two domains: one domain has public value, value that is visible, value that is negotiable, and the other domain has a value that Home Economics is attempting to revalue and to legitimate. But home economists are working against a system that has a 3000 year history of legitimated oppression going for it. As women, we haven't unravelled our history sufficiently to examine these two domains in action and to remind ourselves that whether we speak of practical necessity, or the problems of everyday life, or the perennial problems of human existence, we are talking about a domain that has existed from time immemorial. That domain must be conceptualized so that when we as home economists talk to people outside our field, across this very high conceptual fence, we can make ourselves both heard and understood.

Perhaps female human beings have some intrinsic, inherent hardwiring that draws them to this domain, and that makes it uniquely significant for women. That doesn't mean that there are not men who also find it uniquely significant, but we must recognize that we are in a female-intensive domain. Because the domain of everyday life has been more within the control of women, both the domain *and* women have been devalued.

Defining Two Domains

As we look into the dual domains of the oikos and polis, we must ask, what's the unique purpose of each domain? What would be the goal in each domain? In the domain of the oikos, the goal is to meet the needs of everyday life. What goal organizes activities in the polis? The "common good"? That's one way to put it. You could say common good in the oikos, too. Notice that when we use terminology in one domain, it may not be equally applicable in the other domain. But a commonality exists. Everyone has to eat. Everyone has to be sheltered. Everyone has to be protected from rain, cold, sleet, whether done with clothing or with some other artifact. Both spheres are concerned with food and shelter. But there's a different purpose in the public sphere. As we know it, this domain developed to distribute and maintain social power. Over time, it has taken over some of the activities of the private domain. Today we have huge industries related to food, clothing, and shelter. We have developed service industries. Human emotion and feeling are now treated as "services." They are commodified. The "public good" has been separated from human wellbeing.

If we take the oikos and polis as our "first cut" in organized human life, we gain a different perspective than we do if we accept a one-sided view of human history, the unilateral side of the polis. Under patriarchy, the public sphere was valued over the private sphere. The disciplines of knowledge deal mostly with male ideas about the public world. They have swept the oikos, the private world, out of sight. A lot of public arguments make sense only because they eliminate the household and the family which are "outside" the polis. Somehow this invisible private domain was expected to take care of itself. When things are supposed to "take care of themselves," who does the taking care? Women! Servants! Slaves, both male and female! When work is invisible, devalued, and regarded as insignificant, women are usually doing it. The women's movement is now trying to make some of these activities more visible, but not for the private domain. Day care is a public domain issue and a legitimate one. But we have to deal with it from the proper perspective of the oikos and not from the perspective of the polis. Children in day care return to families. Everything human beings do starts in the private sphere and works out to the public sphere. We must boundary the two domains in our minds. The purpose of the oikos is human survival—survival in all its richness: emotional, physical, mental, spiritual, and ecological. Let's think about the human species in terms of its ongoing needs and remember that all of them, in the final analysis, can be viewed in relation to the oikos as well as the polis. We could say that the family is to the oikos as the state is to the polis. One is the private, personal, domestic sphere; the other is the public, impersonal, political sphere.

The Oikos: The Hestian Domain

In classical mythology (before the time of what we would call "religion") a spiritual *persona* dominated the oikos. She was called Hestia, after the hearth. She was the goddess of the hearth and the goddess of the home. Hestia was Cronos and Rhea's first born, the older sister of Zeus. She was the most powerful goddess, and families were under her protection. She symbolized stability and continuity, essential family values to the present day. She was worshipped in the living flame of the household hearth.

What seems clear is that in the early evolution of humankind there was a focus on fire. Fire represented security and safety. It was a symbol of the energy passed down through the family. Fire might be viewed today as a symbol of the second law of thermodynamics, i.e. of continuity through the transformation of energy. The ancients saw in fire a transformative symbolism: the flow of energy from the physical to the human world. They focussed on the fireplace. What is the fireplace but a place of family connection and communion? Families worshipped their household gods before Hestia, at the household altar. This was not just a pagan superstition. It was a profound spiritual recognition that the human condition was related to natural law. Humans could not violate natural law without destroying the stability, the continuity of the family. Hestia was the peacemaker. It was sacrilege to quarrel in her presence. Hers was a harmonizing, integrating influence.

Through my encounter with Hestia, I found that the idea of Home

Economics goes back thousands of years to a very basic aspect of the human psyche. Perhaps somewhere in the evolution of the species two domains of human action became specialized in human mental hardwiring, possibly in the right and left hemispheres of the brain. Without some intellectual predisposition to work toward ecological wellbeing, we would have been wiped off the face of the earth long ago. The Hestian domain is counter-entropic. Energy is generated. The public sphere is entropic—energy is dissipated! In the public domain our resources are split, dissipated and "used up." In the private domain they may be conserved, recycled, and reconnected.

The Polis: The Hermean Domain

Since I am convinced we must deal with two discrete domains of human action, how can we differentiate the two? We have seen that, in classical Greek thought, the private world was under the protection of Hestia. By contrast, the public world was under the control of Hermes, the god of communication, the protector of bridges, and the god of thieves! In the view of the French classical scholar, Jean-Pierre Vernant, the private and invisible can be viewed in relation to Hestia, the public and visible in relation to Hermes. Each domain had its protector.

Needed: A New Vocabulary

Why is Home Economics invisible? Why must home economists re-empower themselves? The answer comes not from a superficial contemporary view but from one grounded in the thousands of years of the rise of patriarchy, that is, of the institutionalized male dominated polis in which male ideas and male-defined rules have prevailed without the counter-balancing input of ideas and rules from the institutionalized female- dominated oikos.

As a feminist and a home economist, I find feminist theory helpful in explaining our present position. Our devalued, privatized, invisible world, the oikos, became a "separate sphere." The very thing that has happened to women generally has happened to home economists particularly, and even to Home Economics as a profession! Home Economics became what Simone de Beauvoir calls "the Other." The Hermean public sphere is the world. This Hestian private sphere is something else! Such a one-sided view of the world is no longer sustainable. A feminist focus on the public world leaves a vacuum in the private world that only Home Economics is designed to fill.

I think it helps to use the word "Hestian" to describe the kinds of things that occur in the domain with which Home Economics is concerned, to contrast it with the term "Hermean" for the concerns of the "other" domain! This shift in language can help us to communicate. It is hard to define what Home Economics is. Everything you touch is Home Economics. Everything you do is Home Economics in one way or another. Why? Because everyday life is related to the oikos, the Hestian domain. "Our" Hestian perspective is different from "their" Hermean perspective. When your perspective is grounded in the oikos and the Hestian domain, you see one side of the coin of human life. When you look on the Hermean domain of politics, power and economics, the other side of the coin comes into view. If you flip the coin, you cast light on the oikos and the Hestian domain. For the time being, Home Economics has been cast in the shadows for lack of a vocabulary to permit us to communicate what the "other side" is all about. I'd like home economists to practice using this vocabulary as they think about their own vocation. The Hestian vocation is work related to the Hestian domain.

Recapitulate your experience as I have recapitulated mine. I now realize I was exposed to a Hermean education. From the very start Hermean values dominated what I was programmed to accept as of universal significance. Every discipline to which I had been exposed had a Hermean perspective of knowledge. All that time while I was casting about with these little pieces of knowledge, and pursuing everything I was curious about, I was trying to construct the knowledge system for the Hestian domain. That's what Home Economics has done historically, and I think that is where Home Economics is today. Home Economics is the discipline of the Hestian domain. Early on, "domestic economy" was contrasted with "political economy." Under patriarchy, only "political economy" was valued. "Domestic economy" was overshadowed. Women were not allowed to speak in their own voice. They had to echo the voice of patriarchy in order to be heard. Might we learn to communicate more effectively by saying that our concerns are Hestian? This seems perfectly legitimate to me. I am not arguing (as some feminists do) that only women's entrance into public life on an equal footing with men is important. I argue rather that, for a meaningful human life, the two must be kept in balance for both men *and* women. We cannot consistently focus on the public Hermean domain with its power, bureaucracy, dollars, cents and profits at the expense of the private Hestian domain with its human values and commonplace concerns. I hope that this Hestian/Hermean model proves fruitful for further discussion both within and beyond Home Economics.

I'll be glad to answer your questions!

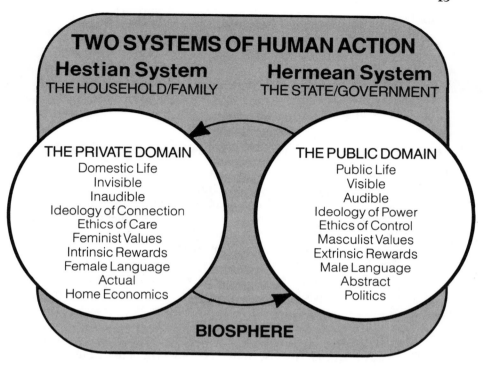

TWO SYSTEMS OF HUMAN ACTION

Hestian System
THE HOUSEHOLD/FAMILY

Hermean System
THE STATE/GOVERNMENT

THE PRIVATE DOMAIN
Domestic Life
Invisible
Inaudible
Ideology of Connection
Ethics of Care
Feminist Values
Intrinsic Rewards
Female Language
Actual
Home Economics

THE PUBLIC DOMAIN
Public Life
Visible
Audible
Ideology of Power
Ethics of Control
Masculist Values
Extrinsic Rewards
Male Language
Abstract
Politics

BIOSPHERE

DIALOGUE

Question: Are you writing a book?

Pat Thompson: I hope to. It will be a theoretical book. We do not yet
have a theory of Home Economics. What I am sharing with you is my
own theory of Home Economics. Most importantly, it has to be a
communicative theory. It has to allow women a way of making the
"first cut" so that, when we talk about our concerns, we are able to ·
look at a public figure as someone who has a legitimate concern with
the Hermean domain and say, "That's okay, but I am a Hestian scholar. I am a Hestian educator. I work in a Hestian discipline, and I am
an advocate for Hestian values." That's a lot easier to get over than,
"Well, I'm an advocate for Home Economics." There's no adjective

for Home Economics. There's no way to say, "Well, that's Home Ecian." I hope that, by drawing on Hestian/Hermean metaphorical imagery and language, we will be able to communicate to "outsiders" what it is we know as "insiders," and do so by using an adjective and not by downgrading ourselves or the other side. The Hestian and Hermean are two sides of the same coin! We can't keep one side up all the time, because if we do we're going to miss the important message on the other side.

Question: To what extent have we excluded men from our domain?

Pat Thompson: I don't think women have excluded men from "their" domain. Food, clothing, shelter, and human connection are not gender-specific needs. They are human needs. Perhaps the problem is the way we dichotomize gender and speak about roles. Roles are Hestian and Hermean but not female and male. Men and women operate on a continuum of "masculinity" and "femininity." There are some very Hermean women, and there are some wonderfully Hestian men. But it's still true under patriarchy that it's better to be an effeminate male than to be a feminist female. "Effeminate" men get a better shake than "feminist" women. That's really a problem because to be "Hestian" is not to be "effeminate" and to be "Hermean" is not to be "masculine." To be Hestian is to recognize and value the private domain. So some of our questions must change, because the gender dichotomy inherent in the concept of "role" is destructive. It distorts our perceptions. We know that men and women follow a very broad continuum of behaviour from masculine to feminine and that there are feminine women and feminine men and masculine women and masculine men. Patriarchal culture has imprinted us with the values associated with specific gender traits. It has universalized the male as norm and "masculinity" as *ipso facto* superior. Most of us are somewhere in the middle with similar traits. If we introduce Hestian and Hermean concepts into our vocabulary, I hope some of these gender-based questions will simply evaporate! In effect, we must carry the debate beyond gender.

Comment: For so long the Home Economics Association has spoken to women. They say "she" and "her." Only recently have they begun to say "she/he."

Pat Thompson: To me it makes no sense to argue about Home Economics in terms of men and women. It makes a lot of sense to argue about Home Economics in terms of Hestian and Hermean requirements in everyday life. Because we need both. We are neglecting this terribly in the States. I won't speak for Canada, not being a Canadian, but in the United States the payoff has been that we have skyrocketing out-of-wedlock births and increasing numbers of so-called single parents. I reject the term. I don't accept that there are single parents. There are just two parents where one parent is absent for one or another reason. We now have to deal with more than two parents. But there are always at least two! So we must reconstruct our notions of masculinity and femininity. Whether we're male or female we must deal with the life of everyday necessity. What has happened under patriarchy is that "everyday" roles have been devalued, and whoever does Hestian work gets the short end of the stick. In ancient Greece it was women and slaves, male and female slaves. So it isn't just a matter of gender. It's a matter of social class and a lot of other factors. When we try to dichotomize on a male/female basis, we end up with the war of the sexes! Home Economics never excluded men. It included men as founding partners. There have always been men interested in Home Economics. They are clearly Hestian men who believe that the domestic domain has value and significance. In the past twenty or thirty years this domain has been ignored, and I think that the feminist movement has to be held accountable for some of that. I say that as a feminist!

Question: Where does property fit in? At one time women were like property. I think we're not out of that.

Pat Thompson: It comes down to the notion of power—of controlling the means of production. There's Hestian power and Hermean power. Hermean power is concerned with control. Women have power too. Women have a lot of power. It's a different kind of power used for different purposes. Women are frustrated in its exercise because we're now in an economy which values only that which can be monetarized. And money has become power. So women become powerless, because women don't earn dollars for their Hestian contributions to the overall economy as child caretakers, wives, homemakers. Hestian contributions are devalued. Hermean contributions are valued. Run for public office and you've got that Hermean thing going for you, but stay home with your children or your aged parents and some people regard that as of secondary importance. That's inappropriate, because outputs from this private domain are essential to human wellbeing in the public domain.

Question: Would you say men dominate because of their greater physical strength, because most men are stronger? Most men do become soldiers, and most men do fight, and they have been able to subjugate women all through the ages.

Pat Thompson: I think there are scrappy little guys, and I suspect it has more to do with their testosterone than their physical size. Because I'm a large woman, I don't think it's a question of size. Little men have tried to treat me as their inferior. I think there are other issues that have to do with who is combative and who is aggressive and the ways aggression is channelled in society. Watch a woman whose child is threatened. You'll see aggression. I could never bring myself to consider myself superior merely on the basis of my size. And I don't think it's reasonable for men to do this, either.

Comment: Right, but it seems that the male, because of hormones, tends to be more aggressive and is physically stronger than the female. Perhaps that has been a factor all through the ages.

Pat Thompson: I've heard that. I haven't seen it demonstrated to my satisfaction. Because some men are big and muscular is not a sufficient reason to kowtow to all men—or even to the big, muscular ones! What about intelligence?

Comment: I remember reading something about so-called pre-civilized society where there was a comment that men were not able physically to lift, to carry as much as women. The comment was, "That's too heavy for a man to do, let the women do it." I think there's something in what women are brought up to do—physical strength is developed.

Pat Thompson: I think we're learning from aerobics that women are better at long-term expenditures of energy and men at short-term expenditures of energy. I'm not in the biological sciences, but we need those data, and we need to know how they fit into modelling this picture. If male-intensive activities are modelled around those biological demands and strengths, then that's something one has to accept and deal with. It's the valuing of those activities that is at issue, not the doing of them. Both kinds of activity are essential for a rounded human existence, but we have only valued those that are public and have become male-intensive, at the expense of those that are personal and have become female-intensive. Each relates to a different aspect of the human condition—and each has value. However, the bottom line for Hestian activity is human survival. It is also the quality of that survival from an aesthetic and ethical perspective.

Question: So you think we've been acculturated into believing that women are physically weak?

Pat Thompson: Hestian or Hermean weakness? There are things men are weak about. Some faint at the sight of blood, or they faint when women are having babies. We have to be more generous and more tolerant. I don't think it is productive to dichotomize that way. That's all part of the old mythology that we have to get rid of because it's really ludicrous. Whether it's the testosterone or the estrogen, I don't know. I really don't care, because I don't value testosterone more than estrogen. Women and men have both. What is important is the preservation of the human race. That's why we have estrogen and testosterone in the first place!

What we in Home Economics must learn to do is validate and legitimate the Hestian domain as a complementary domain to the Hermean domain. When we confront a problem, we have to be able to identify it and say, "You are talking about Hermean issues as opposed to Hestian issues. You cannot keep drawing me into this debate in the Hermean domain because I can't win it. I'm not talking about what you're talking about." When they talk about GNP and women's wage labour and economics, I say, "Wait a minute, when men defined 'economics,' they defined Hestian work out of the picture." It was devalued. We had to make up a new name for Home Economics, although *oikonomeia*, "economics," etymologically goes back to the oikos and the management of household resources. So Hermean patriarchy co-opts Hestian language.

Feminists recognize that language is one of the most important tools of control. When the Hermean domain defines economics, science, politics, and power, think of the hegemony of language which has only a Hermean definition. We have to say, "What kind of power do you mean? What kind of economics do you mean? What kind of science do you have in mind? What are you talking about?" By making a different cut you say, "Wait a minute! We have Hermean concepts over here and Hestian concepts over there." We in Home Economics can say, "When you're talking about Hermean issues — public world issues relating to economics, power, science, and politics — your words tell only half the story. There are two systems in action, but they have different purposes, and those purposes have to be seen as complementary."

For example, that's what Catherine Beecher claimed in different language in the mid-19th century. But her Hestian vision was lost. It was obscured by Hermean language. The feminist literature has been critical of Victorian womanhood and has made a lot of derogatory remarks about "true womanhood" without asking the philosophical questions, "What is 'true' from a woman's perspective?" "What is the meaning of womanhood?" "What is the meaning of manhood?" You can't say that womanhood is deficient because it isn't manhood, *or* childhood *or* adulthood. All this language needs to be reexamined with what I call a "Hestian hermeneutic." We in Home Economics must understand that the language we use is tilted toward Hestian values and toward the Hestian perspective. Others speak in a language where Hermean values and masculist perspectives are assumed to be universal. We have to allow ourselves to discourse intelligently when people come from the Hermean side of this fence. What happened in Home Economics for a good thirty years or so was to try to get the Hermean paradigm into Home Economics so we would all be talking like scientists. Early home economists confronted this by coining the term "domestic science." They were trying to identify the science appropriate for the Hestian domain! But only some home economists are scientists. Just as only some people in the Hermean disciplines are scientists. Everybody doesn't have to be a scientist, or a social scientist. Ellen Richards (an early home economist and a scientist) called Home Economics the "science of right living." Because we have an expanding knowledge base, we have to examine all scientific knowledge from a Hestian perspective. Once I was on the outside looking in. Now that I'm on the inside looking out, I see the Hestian and Hermean domains in their relatedness. They can only be separated arbitrarily. They overlap and interpenetrate all the time. When they are severed arbitrarily, it's to the great disadvantage of the totality of human wellbeing.

Question: Once you get your terms and definitions and so on, I wonder what strategy can you employ. The Hermean side with all the values and the perspectives that are so intrinsic to that domain is probably still going to perceive the Hestian side as not worthwhile or whatever. How can the inroads be made so that this body of knowledge can be an integral part of everybody's education? How can you persuade the people that have the power that that has to be?

Pat Thompson: There are two kinds of power. There are those who have Hermean power and those who have Hestian power. Part of the strength within Home Economics is the ability to mobilize parents and families when children are the issue. We are always perceived as the profession that supports the family. The domain that families inhabit and in which they operate is the household. We have to distinguish between the Hestian space and the living beings within that space. Because the Hestian domain continues, even as families change. States rise and fall. Families rise and fall. Human beings live and die. But the two domains of human action remain the same. I don't think we could ever go back to the single all-inclusive Hestian domain again, as it existed before the rise of the polis. The Hermean domain is there. We have to deal with it. Who knows? In the evolution of the human species something else may pop up some day! Anything's possible. But the question of strategy begins with communicative action. We must develop the ability to formulate the questions and to articulate our concerns in ways that are comprehensible to people who thought they understood or thought they knew what we were talking about, but they really did not. With all the good will in the world, we haven't been able to communicate what it is that we represent. I hope this new language helps. We'll be able to talk more articulately about more complex issues without confusing one with the other. We run into that all the time. We're constantly defending ourselves from this public sphere/Hermean perspective when we have a perfectly legitimate private sphere/Hestian perspective of our own, but no way to explain it. I hope we have it now!

SYMBOLIC REPRESENTATION OF THE HOME ECONOMICS— HESTIAN SYNTHESIS

Artist's Interpretation

Hestia—continuous fire, living flame
Hestia—the centre
Hestia—the gathering point
Hestia—boundaries of soil,
   protecting from chaos and
   chance
Flames—contained and directed by
   hands
Hands—nurturing, creating
Flames—connecting outer circle—
   connection, extension
   into state
Central focus—central universe

1

THE HESTIAN PERSPECTIVE

There is nothing more compelling than the facts of real life. For me, the primary goal is for theory to embrace everyday living.

Ira Shor
A Pedagogy for Liberation.

THANK YOU for a very stimulating evening and questions yesterday. I left excited about the potential of our interchange here. I laid out yesterday (in broad outline) the possibility that we have been thinking in too narrow and gender-bound terms about issues related to Home Economics as a discipline and Home Economics as a profession. I shifted the ground for our discussion from the ground of gender to the ground of human action, and I suggested that we live in two related domains of human action. One is the domain grounded in everyday necessity — in the demands of everyday life. Its purpose is to maintain our biological wellbeing, our social wellbeing, our mental and emotional wellbeing, our spiritual wellbeing and so to maintain the continuity and stability of individuals, families, and the species.

Sometimes we forget that our families are links in the long chain of human development and the evolution of the species itself. These concerns come to mind when we discuss environmental issues. We realize that part of the future of Home Economics is the future of coming generations. It is not just this child in this family at this time, but future children — our grandchildren, our great-grandchildren. Any damage done to the human genetic pool today is going to be fed forward into the future with disastrous results.

So we are concerned about the relationship of the Hestian domain with the natural environment. We might say this concern takes place in a Hestian time frame, different from Hermean clock and calendar time. The Hestian domain is immediate and concrete. But its effects are non-

21

linear and long-term. The Hermean domain is distant and remote. Its effects are relatively immediate.

The Hestian domain deals with things that are "hands on"—things that are within our direct control—things we can manage. The products are visible. But the process of resource management—the oikonomeia of the ancient Greeks—is invisible. The processes by which we manipulate our resources, and the purpose that informs these processes within this domain are invisible to the public world. By boundarying one world as the private, autarkic household domain of the family and boundarying the other as the public, bureaucratic, governmental domain of the state, I am suggesting that there are two different ways of dealing with problems. The Hestian is concrete. The Hermean is abstract. We have to ask whether the very language we use has not become overly restrictive. We have been trying to say things without a vocabulary with which to express the problems that we intuit and that we feel so strongly about. Rather than genderizing and reifying roles, I offer the notion that we deal with two gender-intensive domains, each of which is important in its "differentness." The private household domain has been genderized as female. The public governmental domain has been genderized as male. Those are facts of life. Those are the realities. But they are not ultimate realities. These facts can change. Other realities are possible. Other possibilities must be considered.

We must deal with and sort out human life from an altered perspective that has been implicit in Home Economics from the beginning. Patriarchy has focussed on only one side of the coin of human history. In fact, patriarchy *is* only one side of human history. The male side! Our whole educational history emphasizes one side of the coin at the expense of the other. I drew out of classical studies the word oikos—the Greek word for household. It's the etymological root of the word "economy" which meant the management of household resources. This ancient idea continues in our own mindset toward our Home Economics profession: oikos, the household, ecology, and ecosystem. The family is the changing institution that occupies the oikos, the Hestian domain of the household. We make this distinction because households are unique. They provide the settings for family life. They have a special identity and reality separate from the social identity and reality of the family. The family is a changing institution within the essential domain of human action we recognize as a household. The household domain exists to meet the demands of everyday necessity. It's important to realize that, though we are the profession that focusses on the family, it is the family in relation to a spatial domain called the household—the oikos. The household/family is an ecological unit, a human group and its environment. In Home Economics we call this the family ecosystem.

The private Hestian domain—the family ecosystem—operates in contrast with the public Hermean domain which is the polis of ancient times and the state of modern times. These two domains are in constant interaction. They are not exclusive at all. They exist simultaneously against the backdrop of our natural world, the biosphere. We need to think of them as systems in interaction rather than autonomous spheres. Systems thinking must replace linear thinking for the Hestian/Hermean model to have utility.

Home Economics today needs an embracing metaphor to sustain us in our diversity. So long as the Hestian domain is the focus of the profession, then "Hestian" becomes an adjective rather than a replacement for the name "Home Economics." I have gone from the position of advocating a name change to being adamant about the importance of maintaining the name Home Economics. Experience shows that when the names of departments or units have been changed from Home Economics to human ecology or something else, we have lost our academic integrity and our disciplinary identity. It becomes more difficult to maintain our Hestian identity in relation to the Hermean domain. Patriarchy has made its move! We don't change the name of provinces or states. We don't change the name of our political parties. We don't change the names of things that men have named. Women today like to keep their own family name. "Home Economics" is the family name that integrates Hestian subject matter taken from a number of disciplines. It belongs to us, and we must take pride in it.

The terms Hestian and Hermean are not entirely original with me. My work is built on others' work, but reconceptualized to emphasize its significance for Home Economics. I have told you how I came to be a home economist. Now I'll tell you how I got to be a Hestian!

The French *Annales* historian Fernand Braudel was part of a major intellectual enterprise in France in the 1940s when social scientists tried to bring together Economics, Geography, History—all the diverse social sciences—toward a fuller explanation of the human past, a "global history," a "total history." Understand that these were largely male historians. Their notion was that there was both a visible history and an invisible history. They first used the terms Hermes and Hestia as two personifications of history. Conventional history was likened to Hermes because it was visible. Unwritten history was likened to Hestia because it was invisible. But what they meant by invisible history was the history of textile mills, the history of the baking industry, the history of "lesser" enterprises.

My hypothesis is that women historically have not been part of the discourse that labels such enterprises. As the Annales school of social science developed, it did not have an infusion of women thinkers to say,

"Just a minute, what you're talking about is just another example of patriarchal thinking. There is indeed an undergirding private world, an infrastructure that holds up the public world. The invisible private world of the household and family ecosystem could also be characterized as Hestian." I have made some modifications in the Annales theoretical premise, but so far as I know, this language was first introduced into the social science literature by the *Annalistes*.

Elsewhere I have gone beyond the discipline of history into the psychohistorical and psychological aspects of the Hestian conceptualization. Each re-thinking, I find, reveals more and more the true significance of Home Economics. This is just a disclaimer that I have not invented this out of whole cloth! But I have pieced it together. I have embroidered on it. Everything is derivative. Everything evolves. Unfortunately, women's ideas have not formed part of our intellectual tradition. Men's and women's ideas must be brought into synthesis. Otherwise, patriarchal ideas, Hermean ideas, dominate. Women's ideas have had their evolution interrupted by patriarchy, and Home Economics is a case in point.

Braudel's *The Structures of Everyday Life* is part of a trilogy. Braudel is essentially a medievalist. When I told a colleague I was reading a book by an Annales historian, he said, "I didn't know you were interested in medieval history!" I said, "I'm not interested in medieval history *per se*. I'm a home economist. I'm interested in the structures of everyday life! Isn't Home Economics about the structures of everyday life?" The perennial problems of everyday life provide the conceptual framework for Home Economics. But we've never been able to communicate that to other disciplines. So, I felt that the Annalistes had just half the story, but they certainly do have that! They have other interesting concepts, too. How important it will be for there to be French-speaking home economists interested in this idea, because the Annales historians and French feminists have other notions that would be helpful to us as we continue to explore this idea together.

You will see that the enterprise of developing a Hestian/Hermean way of seeing and communicating must become a collective, bilingual enterprise of discovery. It is not a purely abstract enterprise, because then we're adopting the Hermean mode and losing our connection to Hestian reality. But Braudel speaks about the importance in history of taking a long view, "la longue durée." As we go back in history and examine the evolution of the male-defined disciplines of knowledge, we will see new pieces and fragments of value to Home Economics come into focus through the lens of feminism. It is important for women to know about their history. The history of Home Economics is Hestian history. It must be revaluated from the perspective of "la longue durée."

Feminist Scholarship and Home Economics

Contemporary feminism is in the process of turning history inside out and bringing women into the human story. Again we must avoid the trap of genderized conceptualizations. In adopting the Hestian perspective, we may tease out considerably more that is relevant for women, for families, and for household environments than we would otherwise be able to do. Women scholars are developing feminist Sociology, feminist Anthropology, feminist Literary Criticism, feminist History. A rich tradition is developing—and we must become part of it.

The long term, for me, involves going back to this classical metaphor and penetrating that metaphor to see its relevance for Home Economics. The idea of Hestia is an ancient one. Hestia as the Great Goddess precedes Christianity and has also been alluded to as Earth Mother, Earth Goddess, Mother Goddess. Hestia's goddess image dealt not with generativity in a sexual sense, but with continuity in the species sense. Hestia was worshipped in the living flame of the family hearth. This worship was not idolatry. It was akin to meditation, drawing one into an awareness of one's own agency in the world. We recognize Home Economics as an agency of empowerment. The Hestian model is one of the day-by-day empowerment of the individual through the rituals of household activity. The hearth was the household altar. It was sacred because its flames were used for valued human ends.

As the goddess of hearth and home, Hestia was the protector of household activities. She was, furthermore, a focus for moral decision-making. It is interesting to reflect on what Hestia represented. Hestian symbolism was an early effort on the part of human beings to differentiate two spheres of human action—the private and the public. A life support system of the household existed in the Hestian domain. It involved women, their children, relatives, slaves, servants, and the resources essential for group survival. The emerging Hermean domain of the polis absorbed the energies of men, met their status needs, and became increasingly differentiated and separated from the private domain.

In the anthropological literature we see the significance of fire, hearth, and fire worship. Altars evolved from hearths. The symbolism of fire and the symbolism of the energy embodied in fire can be understood today in a scientific frame of reference. We have moved from the worship of fire to an awareness that energy is the primary source of all life. Home economists deal with transformations of energy in both nutrition and household management today. Energy management permeates our discipline because we deal with transformations of energy in one or another form through our scientific research and through our teaching.

Within this archaic Hestian metaphor there exists the still powerful notion that women, the keepers of the flame, provided the means for basic survival: heat for warmth, comfort, and cooking. Is any language more patronizing to women than "devotion to hearth and home?" Such denigration of hearth and home under patriarchy is something for home economists to ponder. If in early times hearth and home symbolized the epitome of moral agency in human life, what happens to that moral agency when it is reduced to something that seems so trivial? Consider what it meant to keep a fire. Consider what would happen to a human group if the fire went out. Consider that the symbolism of fire was not its inanimate nature, but that in some way it stimulated in the human mind the notion of the fragility and transience of human life. Women's patience was needed to protect and nurture the fire, even as they protected and nurtured people. There was a connection between the technology needed to maintain a fire and a household hearth and the survival of the human family. Why was fire necessary? Not just for food, for warmth, for spiritual observance. It became the symbol of the continuity of the family, of its past and its future. So fire was viewed as a sacred element in the household. We are not talking about idolatry here. We are talking about an internalized spiritual conviction that we are not put on this earth for just the moment. We are on this earth for a larger purpose. We, as women, are particularly concerned about duration because we are concerned with connecting past generations with the generations that come after us, not in the sense of patriarchal domination, but in their wellbeing, in their health, in their normality. When Hestia is viewed as a deity related to the stability of the family, the continuity of the human race, the value of energy, and the need to nurture not only energy but people, we get an image that is infinitely more empowering for Home Economics than anything we can derive from a change of name in a male-defined culture.

So this concrete expression of an abstract idea, of the early notions humans held regarding fire and the fireplace, becomes a way for modern women to see how fire and fireplace moved from the family hearth and altar in the Hestian sphere to public worship in the Hermean sphere. We can see how religion, for example, which once was a family function, has become a public function under patriarchy. I use "patriarchy" as a way of describing the institutionalized sexism that home economists confront as women and as professionals. This should not be interpreted as an anti-male statement. It isn't! It has nothing to do with individual women in their relations with individual men. It has a lot to do with individual women in relation to the institutionalized power that deprives them of opportunities to make decisions or articulate their beliefs with respect to ethics, with respect to aesthetics, or with respect to what is best for children and families. All are concerns in the Hestian domain. Hestian issues deal with real people, real children, real families, real food, real shelter, and real clothing in real situations. In the Hermean domain these issues are dealt with in the abstract, divorced from their effect on real people day-by-day. That's a battle we must keep fighting — against this alienating "rational" principle that distances decisions in the Hermean domain from everyday life in the Hestian domain.

Energy and Entropy in Everyday Life

History shows us that unless women have opportunities to input into the Hermean domain with respect to food, shelter, clothing, children and families, something dangerous begins to happen. Entropy, the dissipation of the true energy of civilization, begins. Hestian tasks are counter-entropic. Sewing up a ripped pair of jeans is not a trivial task. It is counter-entropic. It is a means to conserve resources in which families have invested time and energy. It's a trade-off of the energy of the patch and the energy of sewing to the energy and money required to go and buy new jeans. That is why quilts have so much symbolic meaning. Conserving tasks are not conservative in the conventional sense. They are conservative in the sense of treasuring human value and human actions. The Hestian tasks that we teach in junior high school are counter-entropic: learning to make your own meals, learning to take care of yourself, learning to be well-groomed. Why do people trivialize things that must be done to meet the requirements of everyday life? It shouldn't be so easy to make those things appear unimportant. We can use Hestian language to remind the Hermean world of the significance of the Hestian domain. Neglect of the Hestian domain creates social problems of enormous complexity beyond the ability of the Hermean domain to cope.

Let's think about this Hestian symbol of fire, how fire was kept going, and how much patience and concentration fire-making and fire-tending involved for early humans. Think about what is represented: hunters had a place to come back to, children had a place to stay warm, and women had a place to gather together and begin to create the family unit. Families grouped around the hearth fire. The family's sacred fire maintained its ritual significance into the classical era, the pre-Christian era. One problem Hermeans have with Hestian work is that they want the tasks isolated: give me the cooking, give her the sewing. Give me the child care, you take out the garbage. Take all those things, separate them, then put a dollar value on them! You can't parcel out your whole life this way. To make any sense, these tasks must be integrated toward a coherent human purpose — survival with meaning. As an integrative discipline, Home Economics examines the knowledge essential for these tasks in everyday life and places it in an ethical and aesthetic context.

One thing our Hestian metaphor illuminates is that you must take care of children, feed them, clothe them, all in the same time frame. That's what people fail to see in Home Economics. They see home economists teaching cooking, or they see them teaching sewing. They do not see that these "stewing and stitching" projects help young people to organize their everyday world. Such everyday skills are first steps in ordering the world for one's own survival, to meet one's essential needs without depending on the Hermean world. The Hermean world prevents us from doing that. Instead, it makes people depend on strangers or "the government" for their essential needs. It makes people irresponsible and dependent. People are made helpless. Women resist such disempowerment. They struggle to defend the Hestian domain from being sabotaged by the Hermean domain. Hestian voices are stifled by the rules and strictures imposed by bureaucracies in the Hermean domain. Home economists must learn to be more political, as feminists are. But they must learn to be political in a language that insists on the significance of the Hestian domain. They must legitimate Hestian language.

The Hestian Imperative

Simone de Beauvoir says that women are defined by men and become "the Other." That's a wonderful idea, because you're only "the Other" if you're standing in the Hestian sphere. You're "It" if you're standing in the Hermean sphere! Yet the Hestian concept says we are motivated by the needs of everyday life. That is the Hestian imperative. Home Economics addresses the Hestian imperative—the demands of everyday life—in a structured, systematic way. Home economists have been "otherized," just as women have been "otherized." We have become an "Other" as a profession! Home Economics has been otherized. It has been otherized by both women and men. It is not a profession "by definition!"

Who defines what constitutes a profession? Hermeans define the professions as Law, Medicine, Engineering, the Ministry, and so forth. How can a Hestian profession be defined? Only by hearing the Hestian voice. Home economists "profess" a Hestian mission. Women's voices are rendered inaudible. Their "professions" are ignored. The Hermean world is tuned in only to things it creates and "professes." It's a phenomenological problem. It gets clearer once we realize that we move between two worlds in our everyday life. We must be competent and comfortable in both.

Competence is not just stitching and stirring. To relegate women's total contribution to a practical skill is to diminish it. What about our ideas related to these competencies? What about our views about the moral use of resources? The Hestian mode involves moral agency in the use of human resources. It contains an ethical imperative to use such resources wisely, not wastefully. It embodies both a human and an environmental ethic. The word oikonomeia (which means the management of household resources) is also the root of the words "economy" and "ecology." Management—in one form or another—has been with us since primitive times, ever since women first organized their near environment, the Hestian space around the family fire.

Women established institutions to protect children and sought ways to educate them to become competent human beings. I don't accept that the day-by-day activities from birth to young adulthood are unimportant. We know better. We know that from the very minute a baby is born it is being both physically cared for and socialized. How many actions that were invisible were incorporated into the physical care and socialization of that human being?

We can't allow Hestian history to remain unarticulated because it isn't written history. The Hermean world does all the writing! The Hermean world controls publishing. The Hermean world assigns value to products and services. Look at the artifacts in which women have invested their time and energy. How much symbolic communication goes on in real work and other forms of expression that are devalued!

On the cover of a book that Jean MacKay has in her office is a picture of a stitched sampler. People were always writing in years gone by that girls weren't learning to read, and girls weren't doing this and girls weren't doing that. Where were these girls? They were doing needlework. And what were they doing with their needlework? They were stitching in the alphabet. They were stitching little maxims. They were embroidering mottos. They were learning their numbers. Girls were internalizing the knowledge they needed for everyday life and creating something useful and beautiful at the same time. What is the difference between taking a little piece of thread with a little piece of fabric to make a sampler and reading a printed book? One is empowering to the person as a whole and one is empowering to the mind alone. Hands on is Hestian! It is empowering. So is reading. But they are different. I think by changing, by shifting our perspective somewhat on the history of girls and women, their education and their contribution to civilization, we begin to see that women's contributions are all boundaried by the Hestian imperative.

Systems theory is now coming into Home Economics, but I think it has always been implicit in the field. There has always been within

EVOLUTION OF THE

FIGURE 1: **PRE-CLASSICAL**

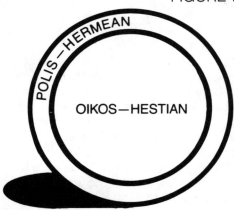

OIKOS, The Household. A self-contained social system in a self-contained bio-system. The kinship group is the centre of social control. Males and females in interaction. Its spiritual centre is Hestia—the hearth.

FIGURE 2: **CLASSICAL**

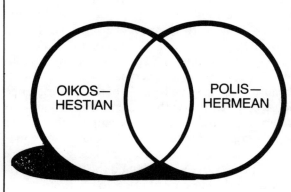

OIKOS gives way to POLIS. The Oikos becomes a private domain. The Polis becomes a city-state. The family occupies the Oikos. A public hearth signifies community in the city state.

HESTIAN/HERMEAN SYSTEMS

FIGURE 3:
INDUSTRIAL AGE

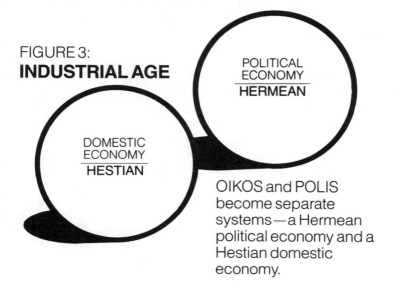

OIKOS and POLIS
become separate
systems—a Hermean
political economy and a
Hestian domestic
economy.

FIGURE 4: **PRESENT-DAY**

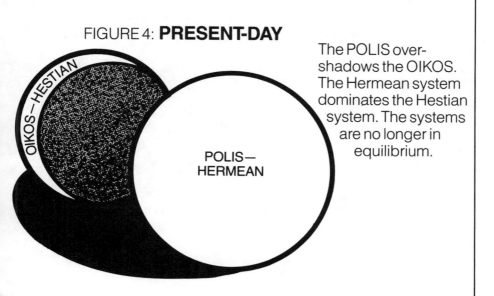

The POLIS over-
shadows the OIKOS.
The Hermean system
dominates the Hestian
system. The systems
are no longer in
equilibrium.

Home Economics a sense of relation rather than a sense of isolation. From the beginning, the Hestian domain recognized and responded to changes taking place in the Hermean domain. Women responded with appropriate household activities and changed interpersonal relationships within the family ecosystem. The Hestian/Hermean model allows us to see a system of inputs, outputs, and feedback loops between the two systems. One can impose the systems perspective on the Hestian and Hermean domains and say they are both open systems. They are interrelated, interdependent, and interconnected. A change in one system will affect the other. The Hermean system may be a little more closed to input from the Hestian system, but it provides outputs. The Hestian system is both open to inputs from and sends outputs to the "other" domain. What it lacks is the power to make effective demands on the Hermean domain.

During the last 20 years, a period that I would call a period of obscurity for Home Economics, it's been difficult to maintain Home Economics as a system of knowledge, education, and action. In the same period there has been a decline of the family as a viable unit, a definite decline in many values we think are significant for the world and the individual's integral humanity. That is not simply the failure of the Hermean world. It is the failure of the Hermean world to recognize and support the Hestian world. And you don't support the Hestian world by issuing welfare cheques. Pouring more dollars into the family system is not the way to strengthen the system. The system is strengthened through education, through reinforcement of family values, and through the recognition that creating human beings takes time. You're not going to get quick fixes in the Hestian domain, because of the length of time that the human being needs to develop humanly. The Hermean sphere is the quick fix arena. You know politicians have two to four years, and that's their time frame. A human life is considerably longer! The Hestian long duration is quite different from the shorter durations of Hermean time frames. Braudel's "longue durée" is a Hermean one. We need a genuine "longue durée" to gain a fresh perspective on the Hestian domain in past time.

DIALOGUE

Question: I'm really concerned, when we talk about the counter-entropic Hestian world, at the difficulty of finding fulfillment there, or allowing people to feel comfortable in that role, when the dollar value is so strong and the Hermeans need to take so many of the Hestian jobs away from the family, who has the strength to really do it?

Pat Thompson: You've certainly expressed it in a way that makes it both clear and problematic. I don't think any individual has that much strength, but I think we have to reinforce our collectivity. What one person can't do alone, a great many women can accomplish collectively. Remember there are also Hestian men, just as there are Hermean women. I think we are positioned strategically as a profession to make those statements. But we don't have very much time (because of the pressures from the Hermean domain) to forcefully regroup as Home Economics was when it was first articulated in the mid-19th century. I know the American history better than the French and English history in Canada; but I suspect that they're not that different, that the world view at that time perfused all of the industrialized societies, and that women, having gained a little leisure after 3000 long years, began to "have it good" in the household. This early direction was lost, I think, by virtue of class differences in the settlement patterns in the two countries. A balance between the Hestian and the Hermean requires truly civilized behaviour, what was once called "gentlemanly behaviour" on the part of men, and we don't have that. We have a lot of meretricious jungle behaviour going on in the guise of politics and business and even education.

Question: Would that not be why the feminist group has used the gender issue as one of the main topics?

Pat Thompson: A good point. Feminists were successful in becoming politically organized. Within Home Economics internationally there has been a kind of low-key organization which I think needs to get energized back to the way it was energized at the start. We have over a 75 year history here in Canada and the United States. That's a long time and something to be reckoned with. People must recognize that we are not a first-generation women's profession. My argument, of course, is that we are a Hestian profession organized to maintain continuity, establish stability, and assure human survival. Those things are not dramatic because they take a long time to accomplish and are hard to see. What people see is the day-by-day stitching and stirring, not the long-run benefits of individual empowerment. Home Economics is for the long term. It is not for the one-shot quick fix. It is also not a dollar fix. It is a human fix.

Question: Could you comment on the feminist goal of day care?

Pat Thompson: When my mother had to work during the Depression, she invested most of her salary in sending me to a live-in day care arrangement. What she didn't know was that the woman who ran the place was sadistic. Her way of keeping order was to beat us. It was just like Charles Dickens. She hired people who were also not trained. One of them told dirty stories to the children. The entire environment had the potential for great damage. I'm fortunate, somehow, that I was born to survive. Around me today are people talking about day care. Where were they as children? I was in day care. I was in the kind of day care for which my mother paid a great deal. She sacrificed so I could be cared for. She had no way of knowing I was being abused. But I was abused. I wasn't sexually abused, but I was emotionally abused, and so were other children.

Now do we want to have, twenty years from now, serious psychological problems because we haven't been sufficiently careful about the kind of day care we provide? We don't plan ahead for it. We don't educate for it. It's simply pulling anybody off the street to become a day care worker. Feminists are not supporting long-term education to provide well educated day care professionals. I don't know about Canada, but in New York all day care workers have to do is have their fingerprints taken, to prove they weren't felons. Then if they *were* felons, they make exceptions anyhow. Because they work cheap. We've seen that happen. We've lived with scandal after scandal about day care. And children can't be advocates for themselves. I tell my students that I think about my own helplessness. I think of my own lack of an advocate, because I couldn't run to my parents. They were doing the best they could in hard times. And that's how many children experience day care.

There are good day care centres of course, but how can we guarantee it? Parents can't guarantee the care of their children at home in the Hestian domain. How can multitudes of parents institutionalize day care in the Hermean domain in such a way that we can ensure the kind of humanizing early childhood education that is essential for a well-balanced adult? It's not easy.

We must look at the problem as Hestian professionals, because if there's any place for early childhood and day care education to take place, it's within the Home Economics university curriculum. It isn't in the Sociology curriculum. It isn't in the Psychology curriculum. It isn't even in the Early Childhood Education curriculum, because that doesn't take the Hestian world into consideration. Public education often Hermeanizes early childhood. Yes, we need day care. We also need feminist support for the education necessary to provide quality day care.

Question: Would you just expand on your comment about Sociology, because it's one aspect that I'm concerned about. Sociology takes in more students, and people say Home Economics is doing the same thing.

Pat Thompson: Let's work on that. I'd hate to have you think I have an answer for everything. But I think when we start to ask the right questions we can come up with better answers. I think that's the right question. Now it's important, once we're able to phrase the question, to then bring our resources into play and consider how to deal with it.

It's because we do *not* do the same thing. The purpose of Sociology is quite different from the purpose of Home Economics. Sociology is a Hermean discipline. It abstracts the human condition. Its outreach—social work—is more Hestian. But there is a major difference. Social work is compensatory and remedial. Home Economics is empowering and preventive.

Let's try to give you something when we come back collectively. I'm not here to just theorize but also to be a facilitator in collective problem solving. I'm not sure I have an instant solution, but I'm happy to hear you raise the question in a way that we can address from our own Hestian perspectives.

Question: How could we apply the Hestian theory here? Right now we're hoping to see a breakthrough in terms of pay equity—getting a fair dollar share. But it's in a Hermean framework and it's also gender-based—the whole approach to pay equity. How can I take your Hestian theory and complement what's going to happen on this side of the ledger?

Pat Thompson: Again, the definitions of "work" are Hermean. The definitions of "pay" are Hermean. In that language, I don't feel it's equity at all. Equity is a more civilized concept than just balancing out "her" dollars against "his" dollars. Equity would introduce the values of the Hestian domain and say, "Maybe we should pay Hestian workers the same amount of money for a six-hour day that we pay Hermean workers for an eight-hour day." Those responsible for Hestian work could leave for Hermean work an hour later and get home to their Hestian work an hour earlier. If women assume Hermean responsibility at work, men should assume Hestian responsibility at home.

Comment: In terms of trying to address the problem in a Hermean framework, which most workplaces are. . .

Pat Thompson: Do you have flextime here?

Comment: Only rarely — very little.

Pat Thompson: I'd be thinking in terms of flextime, because if you get your income within a time frame in which you can manage your Hestian responsibilities, then there is equity in both domains. There's equity in pay and equity with respect to the Hestian domain of family life. The Hermean world does work on linear time. Flextime is more responsive to cyclical Hestian demands.

Question: What would you do if a woman is married to a man who has a drug problem, an alcohol problem, or is inappropriately assigned to take care of children?

Pat Thompson: That is a genuine moral dilemma. One of my students was a nurse. She decided to work days so her husband, a night worker, could be home with the children in the daytime. And she had three little girls. Her husband brought in his drinking buddy for company. When she came home early one day she found her husband had allowed his buddy to bathe the children. That was the last time that happened. But it had been going on for some time. The father and his buddy were drinking beer, and the buddy said, "I'll bathe the children for you." And the mother found that he had been molesting her little girls. You've got to be a realist. Some feminists — Hermean feminists — often provide abstract solutions to concrete human problems. They deal with problems in a Hermean way. We deal with them in a Hestian, connected, unified life-course way. Yesterday's abuse is tomorrow's family problem. Then it becomes a social problem. It isn't necessarily going to be solved by a therapist or a social worker. It has to be dealt with in the now by the family in Hestian time. We ought to look at Hestian education as distinct from Hermean education. Boys have to learn Hestian tasks. We're confronted, as you say, with something that seems almost insurmountable, but as we begin to look at the problems from a Hestian perspective, it isn't nearly as difficult as looking at it from the Hermean perspective. If you try to solve problems from the wrong angle, you get stuck with the problem and become more frustrated.

It may take time for people to get used to us asserting that we deal with a different domain of action and to get that domain legitimated, but it might happen more quickly than we expect, because it does allow us to say that the problems you're talking about and solutions that you are proposing are going to have an impact on the family. That's an impact on the entire Hestian domain which has the needs and demands of the family built into it. The Hermean domain is impersonal. It does not deal with intimate relationships. Hermeans don't want to hear it. What they're going to say is, "Women get so emotional." I do get emotional when children are abused. I get emotional when women are beaten. I get really upset when women are raped. I get emotional when men are abused and mistreated, too. I think it is okay to be emotional. But then my Hermean colleagues (male *and* female) will say, "The problem with you, Pat, is you get too emotional," and I say, "Maybe if you got castrated you'd get emotional too. It's not *your* body. It's not *your* head that people are playing with. Well it's *our* bodies, and it's *our* heads that people are playing with." Don't emotions have a proper place in human life?

Comment: I have a problem with the communication process. We have to use language that will be understood, but we have rules governing understanding, how language is used, and how it's heard. My thing is: a whole lot of hearing aids would be a help! I think there is an unwillingness to hear the message. The message has been proclaimed. Maybe it has been badly done. Maybe it's been without a good solid background theory, but my comment is (and I don't want to be discouraging) I think it's a major obstacle. Unless we communicate in a language the Hermeans can undertstand—and then we're bastardizing our own area maybe—we will not be heard. It's important for it to be heard in that realm. So the rules they use for language and the language they use are not ours. In the process of trying to use language that is acceptable on the Hermean level, we negate ourselves. Something Heather and I were talking about earlier today is that even when we have language which is peculiar to our theme—to our interest, to our concerns—it gets co-opted and used against us.

Pat Thompson: Yes. One of the great contributions of feminist linguistic theory is discovering the way language is co-opted under patriarchy. I guess what I'm proposing is something that can't be co-opted, once we label it. If we have intersubjective meaning for ourselves through this Hestian metaphor, a tremendous amount of power can be generated to open discourse at a different level, to permit us to talk about who we are and what we do at the levels of decision-making. I don't think that is just a vernacular language, I think it is a scholarly language, and I think it is a language of policy where there has never been a "female language" of policy. There is no female language at all, unless we make a decision as a group of committed women in our discipline to legitimate the "different voice" as being a "different language," too. This is my way of dealing with it, and I'm using it now.

One of my students said to me, "Whatever you're teaching, I want to be your disciple." For her, things started for the first time to make sense, and things began to unravel that she found rather tangled. If Hestian language does work that way, and if these two domains of action do represent a new perspective on the human condition, we can bring the language to the thinking world. If we name it, and we claim it, we can begin to discourse in it! The "other" language will fall into place behind it.

We must ask people, "Are you speaking in a Hestian or Hermean way?" Are we dealing with this policy from a Hestian or Hermean perspective; are we dealing with it in terms of control and power, or are we dealing with it in terms of empowerment so that we don't have to spend zillions of dollars at some future time to remedy situations that might have been prevented in the past? The concerns are legitimate. Everything you have said, your reservations about where we are now, anyhow, are legitimate. We're at a precipice. We're reaching a point of no return. Not that I'm a pessimist, because I think that if Home Economics were destroyed, it would have to be reinvented—but at what social cost? The Hestian domain would still be there. Can we allow that to happen? My own moral centeredness says I can't let it happen. One feels helpless sometimes. I don't feel helpless in the company of women. I really don't. I feel that as women begin to focus (the Latin word "focus" means "hearth"), our language provokes a lot of thoughts we have forgotten about. As we focus on certain issues we realize which are the extraneous ones and which are the central ones.

Comment: Faced with a situation where decisions are going to be made regarding course offerings or what would be part of core or non-core, and so on, maybe what we're saying is that it will take a bit of time for us to be heard.

Pat Thompson: True. Language has enormous power to speed up processes, once it's understood. But there has to be a unanimity in its use. Otherwise, we are not communicating. Part of what I hope we can accomplish here is some refinement of the language as we communicate about problems. It is enormously complex to talk about what's happening to Home Economics. When you say "Home Economics," people tune out. Home Economics is Hestian. Some Sociology is Hestian. Some Psychology is Hestian. A lot of Anthropology is Hestian. So is some History, some Biology, some of every discipline! But it's that Hestian synthesis that constitutes the uniqueness of Home Economics.

It seems to me our first order of business is to convince Women's Studies scholars and feminists of our right to be heard by them, and tap into some of their energy—not go it alone but to develop alliances. We must develop some outreach and alliances among these women who are reconsidering what "Woman" and "Family" represent. They are turning back to the Hestian domain. We have the tools to help them. The Home Economics curriculum is a curriculum related to the structures of everyday life. It is the curriculum that can best be reinvigorated by feminist theory and the new women's scholarship. Feminist theory and the new scholarship on women are breaking the Hermean mold.

Women's Studies today is a hodgepodge. What are Women's Studies curricula about? They're trying to break out of the Hermean perspective of the disciplines and turn them around and make them more relevant for women, but they really aren't talking about women. They're talking about the Hestian domain! They're talking about the concerns women have with the environment and everyday life. They are concerned about children. They don't have a language either!

The people we must first persuade are feminists and women scholars, and we have to enter into dialogue with these women. So maybe we must shift our perspective from dealing in obvious ways with the Hermeans. Let's deal instead with the Hestians—both males and feminists. Let's deal with the women first. That might be more effective. If you get vocal women saying all the things we're concerned about, if you can convince them that within Home Economics is the curriculum that they need to reinforce women and children from within, maybe we'll have ready-made allies! We've looked to men to be our allies. We've looked to the Hermean world to support us. Many feminists—like us—are between both worlds. There are some who are strictly Hermean. They happen to be female, and that's where the gender dichotomy proves to be inadequate. There are lots of Hestian males. We can identify them. Certainly in the States, those men who support vocational education have a real Hestian sense of the connection of family to agriculture, because most of them come from strong agricultural areas. They see this connection.

Question: As you're talking about this, I'm just wondering if you have written an article that's been published in feminist magazines.

Pat Thompson: No! I'm not going to live long enough to do that. The first thing that I've noticed with feminists, is that if I say I'm writing in the perspective of Home Economics, they say, "What have you got to offer? You're old fashioned! You're way behind the times! You're holding on to outworn traditions!"

Comment: But I can't see how they would not publish what you write, absolutely not.

Pat Thompson: Well, I have only a certain amount of time to write. My goal is to energize my colleagues in Home Economics to start the dialogue. My belief is that we have to continue to do what we've always done well, which is to synthesize scholarship from the perspective of the Hestian domain. That is a legitimate scholarly enterprise. Now it involves us in synthesizing feminist scholarship. I'm not a quantitative researcher. I don't count noses. I think that synthesis of knowledge from the perspective of the Hestian domain is a legitimate scholarly enterprise for anyone in Home Economics. Women in a variety of disciplines (and men too) are seeing a different infrastructure that we tap into, and that we have tapped into. Every time I read the new scholarship, my marginal notes say "Home Economics," "Home Economics." As I look back at the books I've read, I say "They are talking about Home Economics, but they don't know it." Now I can say they're talking about Hestian issues and Home Economics is the discipline that studies those issues in a systematic way. It works for me. I hope it works for you.

Editor's Note:
For the following discussion, each participant received a copy of a group of cartoons published in Common Ground, *a magazine for Prince Edward Island women, and reproduced in this chapter.*

2

STEREOTYPES VS ARCHETYPES

*Stereotypes of women who do not conform to the
norms and structures of an ideal type of
"womanhood" have depressingly and customarily
depicted them as masculinized, frustrated, bitter and
incomplete. Female society has divided itself, as much
as it has been divided into, matrons and old maids,
wives and spinsters, mother and the childless, a
division perpetuated as much by women as by men
whose contempt for non-conformist and single
women is well documented. At worst they are
stigmatized; at best they are a half told joke.*

Patricia T. Rooke,
Women: Images, Role-Models.

BY GOOD LUCK, just before we met in Rustico, my attention was
called to these wonderfully funny cartoons which had been published in
Common Ground. They convey the stereotypical views of women that
women deal with in feminist consciousness-raising. Consciousness-raising for home economists is important, too. Stereotypes are, of course,
ways to put down women. We could add "home economist" to the list of
stereotypes, couldn't we?

No woman can have lived into her adult years without hearing herself
or other women stereotyped in one or more of these ways. Seeing ourselves this way can make us angry. We must tease out of these familiar
"put downs" some aspects that could be related to our emerging Hestian
consciousness. We can make the distinction between a stereotype and
an archetype. Stereotypes turn women into objects. They are degraded
versions of women's power, a power once personified in the "First Goddess," Hestia. I have proposed, as have Jungian analysts, that there may

be a Hestian archetype "hardwired" into our psyches. Rather than being a stereotype of women's "traditional roles," there may be an archetype of women's orientation.

The Bride

Let's look at The Bride first. To become a bride is to become a man's ideal. The bride has become an insipid stereotype.

In our university a lot of mature women are coming back to college. When I teach family relationships, a good many women in my classes have been married, maybe once or even twice, and some have had disastrous experiences because they're left with children to support. Some of them are unmarried. Yet this bride image is still hard to shake. Very hard. Women buy into the notion of passivity, perfection, and purity. Women—even those living with their boyfriends—really want to get married. That's how powerful that image is. Part of the stereotyping process is internalized throughout our lives. We accept these images uncritically.

One of the exciting things about some of the current work in Home Economics is critical theory, the idea that we can't take every assumption without examining it and saying, "What does this mean?" Now I'm trying to add this Hestian level to critical theory and say, "In Home Economics, critical theory is going to be a Hestian critique of the Hermean world." Incidentally, feminist scholars (as a group) are not at that level yet. They are not at the level of critical theory. They are not at the level of thinking about meaning, because they can't. They only have Hermean categories to work with. Even those doing interdisciplinary work haven't yet caught on to the fact that sooner or later they're going to be putting these disciplines together, and it will explode some of the Hermean myths that we have been living with. That isn't to say that getting married and establishing a family isn't one of the most important Hestian works in the world. The point is to substitute the reality for the romanticized image. And we can't continue to let female children buy into the notion that once married everything's going to be just wonderful! Some end up in shelters for battered wives.

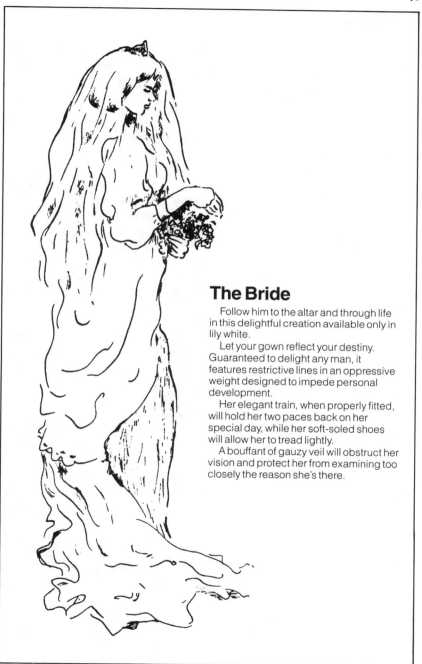

The Bride

Follow him to the altar and through life in this delightful creation available only in lily white.

Let your gown reflect your destiny. Guaranteed to delight any man, it features restrictive lines in an oppressive weight designed to impede personal development.

Her elegant train, when properly fitted, will hold her two paces back on her special day, while her soft-soled shoes will allow her to tread lightly.

A bouffant of gauzy veil will obstruct her vision and protect her from examining too closely the reason she's there.

Barefoot and Pregnant

Let's look at the next image. Here we are, Barefoot and Pregnant. Once a woman becomes a mother, she's confronted with an awful lot of unanticipated work. The kids don't realize that babies create dirty laundry. These beautiful babies that they imagine coming into their lives never mess up a diaper, never spill on their bibs, never wake up in the middle of the night and throw up all over their mothers. The work of the household created by the process of living is Hestian work, not "housework" or "mother's work." It isn't disembodied "abstract" work, which feminists talk about. Housework isn't disembodied. Its purpose is to support the essentials of everyday life—the life process. You've got disembodied socks, disembodied shirts, and disembodied pants. These items all belong to people, and they're all part of everyday rituals, part of getting it together. They get mismatched and mislaid. That's entropic. They get washed, matched and put back. That's counter-entropic. We have to name the Hestian processes we are involved in and that we know are essential. Jobs that are disembodied from the rest of the jobs of the household are alienated labor. Hestian labor becomes Hermean. That's alienating. Buying a washing machine or drier invites buying more clothes and doing more wash. That's why Hestian work is never done and why we have to ask ourselves the purpose and value of Hestian work. "Housework" is made work. It is pointless, meaningless, and repetitive. Hestian work has a point, a purpose, and a meaning. It is tied in with Hestian time, not Hermean time. It is tied in with Hestian values and the goals of human wellbeing and species survival.

The nature of everyday life is that socks get dirty and dishes get dirty. It comes to the point where you want to simplify. You want to say, "What is the purpose of all these material possessions—these labour-saving devices—that are occupying our time and our lives?" That was the question of "household efficiency" as the early home economists perceived it. The goal of Home Economics initially was to make household work more "efficient" so as to leave women free for higher pursuits, for moral and spiritual "uplift" so they could meet that inner need human beings have to make sense of the world; not to use up every bit of women's energy and time so they're so bushed and beaten and tired there's nothing they can do but turn off the TV and the washing machine and go to bed. For a lot of women that's the end of the day; just to do the mechanical operations and fall into bed exhausted and get up the next day with no energy for the more profound aspects of human life.

Women have a lot to contribute to "philosophy." Women have a lot to re-examine. Women in religion today are asking some of the same questions home economists have asked in a secular framework: What are the

Barefoot and Pregnant

The little woman will glow in these red hot pants by "Bun in the Oven".

Intended to be worn in bare feet, they allow maximum agility and traction as you race through your challenging schedule.

The clever design of this loose-fitting top provides comfort while setting you apart from those bra-burning radicals as a real woman.

The obvious accessory to this ensemble is, of course, the laundry basket—the only vessel large enough when filled, to provide the necessary ballast.

Hair curlers frame that satisfied look.

moral obligations of being a female human being? Is it to do laundry? Is it to become pregnant? Are those moral obligations? Or are these actions simply a part of the necessities of species survival?

The Good Mother

How long does it take for mothers to get disenchanted? The Good Mother! How do you define the good mother? Biology is destiny? What is a good mother? Stereotypically it consists in serving someone else, putting someone else ahead of your own needs. That is the traditional view. Evelyn Duvall did a wonderful analysis of what a good mother is from both a traditional perspective and a developmental perspective. The developmental parent is different from the traditional parent. I think in Home Economics we internalize the notion of the developmental parent, the parent concerned with the child's wellbeing, but we also have to reintroduce and certainly vindicate that the parent has some right to development too.

Women don't have the time to examine what they are doing because their lives are punctuated. By that I mean that they are constantly being interrupted. Hermean time—clock time—is linear. It breaks up Hestian time, which is cyclical. As good mothers we tried to give meaning to our children's lives. In later life, we're responsible for giving meaning to the closing decades of our own lives. We don't have institutionalized supports for that. We have no way of formally passing along the collective wisdom of women. Under patriarchy we pass along the collective wisdom of men! It is a matter of what Carolyn Hunt, an early home economist, called "revaluation." We have to rethink what we mean by "good mothers," and "good fathers," and "good homes." As home economists, we revaluate in every decade without being aware of it. We have talked about changing sex roles because we don't have more precise language. That language is inadequate. Hestian demands require Hestian responses. Those responses are not sex roles. Hestian demands are placed on us by virtue of our existence as human beings. You can't abrogate them. You have to revaluate them.

Question: How do gender roles fit in?

Pat Thompson: When we talk about gender roles we get drawn right into the notion that there is something ineluctable about being male or female or that society makes those determinations consciously. When we talk about Hestian demands, people will have to say, "If we're going to arrange for food, clothing, shelter, and family, we're going to have to have some knowledge for that. But where are we

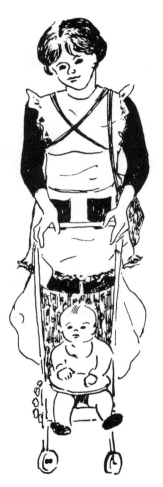

The Good Mother

A must for every good mother, Christine models this dual-pocketed, wash'n'wear protective top, designed to withstand children.

Running shoes enable her to make music, swimming, dancing and gym lessons on schedule, while her back-pack provides room sufficient for chauffeur and membership cards. Diapers, snacks and a variety of entertainment aids can also be accommodated in this handy carry-all.

Also, the stroller, her indispensable accessory, provides areas around and under baby, as well as from the handles.

A good mother recognizes that she owes her physical and mental fitness to her children's activities — which also gives some meaning to her life.

going to get it?" And that's where we come in and say, "This inaudible voice is going to be heard—it's inaudible because the questions haven't been asked in a way that demands an answer." And it may be that, with the help of feminist thinking and scholarship, we will be able to pose those questions differently. Then, with the new knowledge we gain, we may modify our concept of good mothers, good fathers, and good children. That's certainly difficult today—to define what a good child is. For example, some of us raise sons by ourselves. I said once to one of my classes that women raise the sons they would have wanted for husbands. I suddenly realized that it's often true. My son is my ideal man. Somehow I raised the ideal man for someone else. So you project into the future what it is that your own internalized values determine in your day-by-day child rearing.

Debbie*: I have a daughter, and she's much more maternal than I am—much more the mother type. Because I worked all the time she was growing up, I often ask myself if that's why she devotes herself to her children so much—

Pat Thompson: That's interesting, because I could say with self revelation that my son didn't function well in the Hermean role. He was too thoughtful about women. One time he called his secretary "my girl" and I went right off the wall, and he said, "Mother you don't understand what it's like in that office. I can't do what they're asking me to." After three jobs in a law firm he had to work from home. He could not function in the Hermean world and its values, so he had to become an independent practitioner.

The Mother-in-Law

The Mother-in-Law stereotype is a curious one in our society. The very word invites cheap shots at humor.

Ellie: In our society there is no word for addressing one's mother-in-law. When you are first married, you call her "Mrs. Jones." Then when a child is born, you call her "grandma." Our society does not have a word to express the mother-in-law relationship as many cultures do.

---

* For anonymity, participants of the Belcourt Conference are identified, hereafter, with randomly assigned first names.

The Mother-In-Law

For the uncompromising mother-in-law, this suit creates an authoritarian presence, cut of black polyester in the ever-popular tuxedo style.

A no-frill, no-nonsense, pristine blouse accentuates the lines of the jacket, while the priceless heirloom broach provides that unmistakeable insignia of rank.

Good Housekeeping and The Holy Bible form part of her accessories — at the ready to defend any statement she makes, should one be so foolish as to challenge her.

Her head is crowned with a tidy hat and her feet encased in sensible shoes to allow her to run interference.

Barbara: My children-in-law both call me "Barbara."

Ellie: Yes, sometimes they do, but that doesn't express a relationship does it?

Pat Thompson: In the Jewish tradition the relationship of in-laws has a name. In-laws become "machetunem." We are really bereft in terms of names for relationships. When your child marries someone, that person's parents have a relationship to you. That was a revelation—that there is a culture that actually designates that relationship. I thought that was a lot more civilized than what some other cultures do.

Ellie: We handle it by joking. We take the structure of family life from the perspective of white, Anglo-Saxon, Protestants so much for granted that we never take an anthropological view of family structure and realize that we could arrange things differently. Mothers-in-law could have names; a mother-in-law could have formal rights or functions.

Pat Thompson: We are beginning to fight for grandparents' rights in the States. I don't know about Canada, but following divorce where children are involved, grandparents have stood up for the right to see their grandchildren. The Hestian domain is cross-cultural. We are all members of the same species. Cultures define different family structures. Because families are changing, rights, duties and responsibilities in the Hestian domain are changing, too. Roles are changing. The Hestian institution of "the family" is changing, even as we speak! What doesn't change are the Hestian demands of everyday life that families are structured to meet.

Someone yesterday was speaking about a marriage here, where a fellow had been divorced, and characterized it as a civilized divorce because the ex-wife and the wife were both concerned when that man died. This is civilized. But what we are seeing a lot is people who are competing for loyalties. It's terrible because it damages children. The fact is that in the Hestian domain, the demands of everyday life remain. We change the institution—through divorce, remarriage, open adoption, surrogate mothers—all kinds of changes in the relationships of families. Some are pretty bizarre. Change in the family within the Hestian domain doesn't change the need for food, clothing, shelter, child care and family connectedness. The structures of everyday life remain the same. Governments change: the state remains. It's the same thing. These changes can get a little perplexing!

Being a mother-in-law is a really profound thing because, if your children divorce, you will still have a set of connections with your former daughter- or son-in-law. You should have a right to maintain that relationship. And yet we have such exclusive notions about human relations and ownership. We have to re-examine the idea of "people as property." It is not in the best interests of the Hestian domain. Women have to—and women do—make those decisions ultimately. They decide who gets invited to parties. They decide who gets invited to weddings, christenings, and other family events. In many cases we have to assign that task to mothers-in-law! They are the repository for a lot of family wisdom. My mother-in-law had a lot of wisdom, and when I had difficulty with my marriage, she was the one who made room for my son and kept family rituals and birthdays—memorable occasions—going. She didn't let us fall apart as a family. And that was the counter-entropic emotional work she was doing as a woman in the Hestian domain. She was a Methodist minister's wife, so it was hard for her to deal with divorce and that sort of thing. But women do that. Women do mediate change in relationships. It happens at an individualistic level, not at an institutional level. It is too threatening to patriarchy's Hermean view of people as property.

Poor Little Girl and Selfless Companion

Pat Thompson: What do you think of that? This one I find troublesome. How do you react to it?

Sonya: I think it's just another example of devaluation. The physically handicapped person has been devalued and depersonalized. She doesn't have the dignity to become womanly. Wrap her up warm and tote her around.

Ellie: Pity the poor elderly person.

Pat Thompson: We treat older women like little girls!

Sonya: Ask the person with me what I want to eat!

Sandra: I think invisibility is characteristic of this whole area. People don't want to look at, don't want to see a man or woman in a wheelchair or with any kind of disability. They pretend they are not there.

Sonya: Very successfully sometimes.

Sandra: Because they don't know how to deal with it. We know that someone has to deal with it. We know that the demands of everyday life are such that given these circumstances someone has to pick up the pieces and do something human. And yet it's not respected, it's not seen, it's devalued. So it's another kind of emotional counter-entropic work to be a healer, to be someone who's concerned. The feminists have done a wonderful job in bringing these issues into consciousness. They have had a major role insisting on access. They have been very vocal in terms of recognition of the needs of the handicapped as human beings.

Pat Thompson: Feminists' meetings are excellent, for instance, about day care. I don't think I have ever been at a Home Economics meeting where day care was provided, never. But at any women's group meeting, day care is provided, special facilities for the handicapped are provided. I don't know that we do that. Yet in our teaching, we are aware and we incorporate it as a concern in our teaching model. But I don't know that we do so in our institutional model, in 4H, in our public displays. . .

Debbie: Canadian Home Economics Association over the years and in the provinces have provided day care.

Pat Thompson: I'm so glad to hear that.

Wendy: There was a babysitting service at the conference in Ottawa, and I think there was something in Saint John.

Ellie: In planning for this workshop it never entered my head, and I'm a feminist. Here's a woman who would have brought her daughter if care had been provided. We are always strapped in our thinking, really we are. . .

Trudi: Just to be the devil's advocate: Sometimes I wonder why we have day care for women's organizations when men don't offer day care at their organizations. And I think sometimes, making day care part of the meetings just means that the women end up with two jobs. They still take their children and are concerned about them. I know the other way they still have to make some kind of arrangements for the children. But I have a problem with saying day care should be offered to women's group meetings.

Ellie: They have just finished a veterinarians' conference here, and I think that they provided day care or some kind of care for children or entertainment for children. Here again we come back to the question of which are the well-to-do meetings. Here we are doing this on a

Poor Little Girl and Selfless Companion

Susan models for us street wear for the physically handicapped.

Nighties of flannel are ever convenient—easily donned and maintained—for people who don't care what they wear anyway.

Yellow slippers and multi-coloured afghan complete her attire.

Please note, colours need not be co-ordinated as it's not as if anyone will notice. All people will see is their dear, sweet faces—they won't dare look beyond.

Pat, her selfless companion, looks stoic in her robe of saintly white. Her colourless countenance is a mirror of despair and martyrdom.

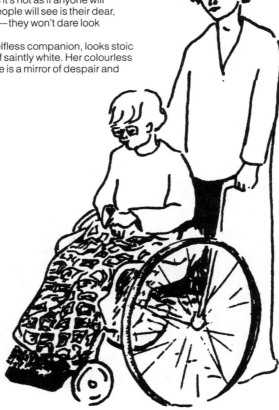

shoestring, and the veterinarians would have a lot of money to spend on their conference. I think there is a difference here because we are a women's organization.

Pat Thompson: I see that special bind that you're in. Hestian demands have to be met. Children have to be taken care of. If we leave our children, somebody has to be responsible for them. But we don't institutionally assume that responsibility, although part of the Hestian domain, what we teach about, is to the children's benefit. But it is a double bind. Bear in mind that the Hermean world's purpose is to maintain patriarchal power through control of human and material resources. Women are a resource. Money is a resource. Caring for the handicapped is a Hestian concern. Maintaining human dignity is a Hestian ideal.

Why? Because that is how we survive as human beings!

The Superwoman, The Old Maid, and Others

Pat Thompson: Let's discuss The Superwoman and The Old Maid. The Superwoman is the compendium of everything "now," and don't we all expect to be superwomen?

But the Old Maid. What is the meaning of that?

Peggy: I just want you to know before we start—I was the Old Maid (for the cartoon) and I didn't know you were using this.

Pat Thompson: Why did they pick you? Did you write this?

Peggy: I sort of wrote the text!

Sandra: I think old maids say something to me that's very negative—that you really don't belong or you can't be a full person unless you are intimately connected to some man. So because you're not full you're constantly yearning for that, kind of. It's a negative way of saying I'm incomplete, I'm available. My clothes don't show it, but that's a put-on.

Pat Thompson: Is it implying that because you are not attached to a man you're a loser?

Sandra: Yes. A loser and incomplete. I find that every once in a while it crops up, "Oh, you're not married." You're left behind in some way in your life. You're a leftover being because you don't have that connection to a man.

Superwoman

takes a job
makes the meals
keeps the house
does the shopping
raises the family

Old Maid

Hope springs eternal in this simple frock by Missionary.

Heather's one-size, go-anywhere, all-season has been embellished with virgin collar and genuine, simulated pearl buttons.

Lyle stockings provide warmth while she waits for the heat of a man's touch.

Thick glasses will enable her to burn the midnight oil reading true romances, so she'll know how to respond "When it happens".

Black purse and heavy black shoes complete this virtuous yet unassuming look.

No obvious style, this costume should appeal to any audience—god willing!

Peggy: Then because you're not connected, there's no man in your life to check on your opinions and to keep you in order.

Sandra: But Old Maid is in line—Old Maid is not an image of one who would upset any applecarts.

Ellie: She's not a temptress.

Sandra: No, and she's not considered somebody who has original ideas.

Ellie: Or credible. She's kind of left over.

Sandra: Left over from the market.

Paula: I think Old Maid is an old fashioned thing. I don't think there are any Old Maids today. I think of Old Maids as something from my childhood maybe. But Old Maids? There's no such thing! I don't know where these Old Maids have gone.

Wendy: Swinging bachelor girls are in!

Pat Thompson: When you read about Hestia, it is not uncommon to find her described as an "Old Maid." It is true she never married, but she had two suitors. She turned them down. And they were "good catches," too. But she chose to remain alone. I believe there is something in this stance that is far more profound at an existential level, and our discussion of the "Old Maid" stereotype has gotten to it. Also, we have to deal with the connotation of "virgin" as woman "untouched by man," which defines woman only in relation to man.

Then you have to consider the mythology that says women defile men on contact. Patriarchy has passed down some very dubious ideas to us. That is part of The Temptress stereotype.

We should also look at the idea of the Gossip. That is a put-down of the way women communicate. They often challenge the status quo when they engage in "gossip." They see through pretense and hypocrisy. Gossip is the way powerless and oppressed people get their message into a hostile system. Is it really so bad? Not all gossip spreads lies! It often exposes lies, however.

The Bag Lady is the most tragic figure to me. She is the woman whose Hestian space has been taken from her. She may try to "stake out" a space in a doorway or bus station. We see many homeless women on the streets of New York. It is a symbol of the ultimate tragedy for any person—to be totally deprived of place, to be without any true connection in the world. It is the ultimate failure of society when we tolerate their presence in Hermean space and turn our backs

Temptress

Ann lures attention in her siren-cut gown (also available in decoy red).

Her generously scooped bodice is tastefully balanced by the full-length skirt—punctuated by peek-a-boo slits.

Jewelery by Gold Digger provides that finishing touch—complementing her ensemble, while reflecting the hungry look in her eyes.

This woman means business and, of course, your pleasure is her business.

The Gossip

Although offered in a variety of weights and colours, the traditional gossip garb can boast a long and pure history.

Only styled for women—as men don't gossip—this costume has never offered trousers. Both full and street-length skirts are popular.

Shoes must be thick-heeled to comfortably run around the neighborhood to circulate rumours.

Wisps of lace at the neck will assist in veiling the truth while the professional pin, strategically positioned, will lend credibility as she spreads her tales.

The Bag Lady

Designed with the "downtown" woman in mind, Jean sports a creation of necessity.

For the homeless woman on the move, the layered look is the obvious answer.

Crowning layers of sweaters and vests, an oversized great coat provides ample storage for all of life's little necessities.

Running shoes are all-important as one may have to move on quickly, while shopping carts are optional accessories.

on it, forgetting that "There, but for Hestia's grace, go I!"

Some say that The Witch is a degradation of the Hestia myth. When the spiritual dimension is lost, we are left with the idea of women's power as something evil and frightening—not something good and empowering.

In The Dizzy Blonde stereotype we have the idea that women may have physical beauty—but not brains—and certainly never in the same package. Then it is implied that to be beautiful is better than to be brainy.

Of all the stereotypes, The Women's Libber is probably the worst of all! She actually wants to get out from under all the heavy messages of patriarchy. She wants to strike out for herself. She wants power. But the dilemma is—does she then become Hermean? We need to break away from all our gender stereotypes and think about our common human ground.

SUMMARY

The so-called Old Maid is defined by a Hermean definition of what the woman is, in, of, and by herself. But how would women define a woman who is centred in her female being—one who is truly centred in being female, in recognizing her female view of the world? How would we define a woman who is centred in being female? And what power would that definition bring to the world if we could release it? What does Hestia represent? A centreing in herself, not selfish, but centred in being female, and centred through connection with an intimate human group. From the centreing view of the Hestian domain, a woman is going to look at the world differently. Why can't a woman look at the Hermean domain and say, "My being centred in the Hestian domain is my strength, not my deficiency?" Every definition of the female centered in the Hestian domain is a male-defined image. Maybe home economists are perceived as kind of psychological Old Maids. They aren't making inroads in the Hermean world. They haven't got "what it takes" to be out there where it matters and to get the Hermean rewards that are there to be had for those who are successful, assertive, and effective. Maybe it's because, in some female-defined way, they have a positive affinity for the Hestian domain and the "connectedness" it represents.

The idea I want to leave with you is that we must move from stereotype to archetype. We must move from degrading to upgrading the *idea* of woman.

The Witch

Fly anywhere in the warm, earth-tone-and-splinter-resistant skirt created especially for late nights and cool temperatures.

These smart, dainty shoes featuring pointed toes will allow you to kick up your heels and raise a little hell.

That devil in your life will love you in this charming hat, delicately embroidered with traditional good-luck symbols — also available in styles to complement your pointed shoes.

And finally, cast a spell in this magical cape offering convenience and style. A place for everything and everything in its place — organize your food stuffs and magic potions easily in its multi-pocketed lining, perfect for the avid collector. This innovative item could allow you to dispense with cumbersome handbags forever.

The Dizzy Blonde

Party, party in this cute little number designed to impress even the intelligentsia (you know, people who work in libraries and museums).

Critical is the length of skirt which must never allow for bending or stooping.

The perfect co-ordinate for this slinky little jersey is the rodeo top which will allow you to "round 'em up" and "head 'em out".

Misty mauve hose drawn over miles of leg elevated to tippy-toe, will take his breath away, and lots of jewelry will facilitate fascinating conversation as you reveal how you came to own it.

Women's Libber

Perfect for the "woman against everything", our basic "protest wear" line has been expanded to include contemporary accessories.

We continue to offer the ever-popular cullotte, providing freedom of movement while distinguishing mommy from daddy.

The army-green jacket affords the perfect backdrop for protest buttons and a suitable fabric from which to suspend children and accessories when the baby sitter fails to show.

T-shirts are now available offering a variety of multi-purpose messages including: "Remember, we beat City Hall".

Especially recommended for the light weight these steel-reinforced boots are all-important in your war to squelch contradicting opinion.

THE SEVEN GODDESS ARCHETYPES
(as identified by Shinoda Bolen)

ARTEMIS

goddess of the moon and hunt, personifies the independent, achievement-oriented feminine spirit;

ATHENA

goddess of craft and wisdom, represents the logical, self-assured woman ruled by her head rather than her heart;

HESTIA

goddess of the hearth, embodies the patient and steady woman who exudes a sense of intactness and wholeness and finds comfort in solitude;

HERA

goddess of marriage, stands for the woman whose essential goal is marriage, and whose role as wife takes precedence over others, such as student, mother, or professional;

DEMETER

the maternal archetype, represents a woman's drive to provide her children with physical and spiritual sustenance;

PERSEPHONE

the child-woman, expresses a woman's tendency toward compliancy, passivity, and a need to please and be wanted by others;

APHRODITE

goddess of love and beauty, the embodiment of sensuality and sexuality and the striving to fulfill both creative and procreative roles.

3

THE HESTIAN ARCHETYPE

Knowledge has been overwhelmingly male in subject matter, in assumptions, in methods, in interpretations . . . a disproportionate share of human knowledge has dealt with a world viewed through a male prism . . . not only equity but also the human legacy calls for a correction of this situation.

Jessie Bernard
The Female World.

LET'S MOVE FROM the idea of the stereotype to the idea of the archetype. When Jung conceived of the archetype he thought of it as what we might now call the "hardwiring" of the human psyche. It is a psychic pattern imprinted genetically that we strive unconsciously to achieve, to fit ourselves into. Jung saw the archetype as something primal in our human mental apparatus. He postulated the *anima* as the "feminine" side of the human psyche and the *animus* as the "masculine" side of the human psyche. Anima and animus co-exist in men and women, both mentally and emotionally. Jung's work was so different from Freud's because it was more intuitive and more mystical. It was less patriarchal. Some feminist psychologists and psychotherapists have tapped into Jung's ideas.

Women will recognize that they possess more than one of the archetypal behaviour patterns and its personality traits. Whereas stereotypes label and confine women, awareness of the archetypes arouses in women the range of possibilities inherent in being a female human being.

Jean Shinoda Bolen, a Japanese-American psychiatrist, in a book called *Goddesses in Everywoman*, identified several archetypes for women. The archetypes Jung had described, such as the trickster and the magician, were generally male. Hermes, by the way, is also the archetypal trickster. Jung's archetypal theory, as interpreted by feminists, emphasizes the anima. That is the part that relates to our "feminine" inner gyroscope. Bolen proposed a set of archetypes for women drawn from classical Greek mythology.

There were three "virgin" goddesses — three Old Maids! Who were the three unmarried goddesses? Hestia, Athena, and Artemis. What did they do with their lives? Hestia was the first-born of Cronos and Rhea, the single most important Olympian goddess. Athena, born from the head of Zeus, was the goddess of wisdom. Artemis was the athlete, the huntress. We try to tap these archetypes into the stereotypes — the archetype of The Temptress is Aphrodite, the love goddess. The goddess Hera, whose goal was to maintain her marriage to Zeus, was forever worrying about her husband. She is the archetype of the matron and the wife. Demeter was the goddess of agriculture, mother of Persephone. She is the archetypal mother, forever concerned with her child's wellbeing. Persephone, the errant daughter, maintains her connection with her mother over lovers and husbands.

Bolen describes Hestia and uses the imagery of hearth and home to portray the woman who likes to be at home, and she talks about housekeeping tasks. If women were to abstract the notion of housekeeping, it would be the ordering of personal space. Housekeeping becomes the ordering of the private domain where resources essential for the maintenance of human life are collected, stored, and distributed — the classical definition of "home management." We let people race past Home Economics and say it's about "housekeeping" instead of saying back, "What is housekeeping?"

The question "What is housekeeping?" can be a philosophical question, just as much as the question of what is the sublime, the beautiful and the good, philosophical abstractions created by male thinkers. Women can raise philosophical questions about the Hestian domain, about everyday life as they know it. I've looked into my own self as a Hestian person, and I think about the tasks that I do in my life. I am a very organized person by some standards. In fact, it seems I sometimes create disorder to recreate order. I do that when I paint, write, prepare a meal — undertake any project. The archetypes have all emerged at one time or another in my life. Until the feminist movement, however, I could never take pride in woman-defined imagery.

What might have happened if, instead of having them created for us by others, women had created all the categories of human thought? What if women had created the gender frameworks in which we live? What might they be? Would Hestia be the generator of these alternative conceptual frameworks? I suspect we have within us as part of the anima and our female archetypal needs, a gyroscope that wavers until we find our way into a Hestian place. If allowed to do so, we would construct things differently, and there would be categories that haven't yet been designated. We would establish and recapture as concepts what we as female human beings intuit or sense. We would break some categories and combine others. A lot of the concepts we work with day in and day out in our professional lives are ill-fitting and ill-suited to what we see and think are primary. I'm certain our priorities would differ. The priorities in the Hestian domain are more than a simple reverse of Hermean priorities. It's not matriarchy versus patriarchy. It's a revaluation of purposes and of priorities from a Hestian perspective articulated by women.

DIALOGUE

I'll give each of you a different piece of my research notes. Would each group pick one central issue you think is important for us to think about together? Identify what seems to be a major issue. Come back and tell the others. If we don't have solutions, maybe we can find new ways of framing questions that we can carry with us for the future. I'd like you (the French-Canadian women) to form a French-speaking group, so you can take the French language material because you have something important to contribute to your colleagues. You can translate and disseminate some important ideas for those of us who do not speak or read French. We can all benefit from this exchange.

Please identify your group in your report so we'll know who to turn to later for expertise!

Group One Report

Anna: We were the French group. You gave us the French article by Martin. I am from Saint John, New Brunswick. The point we would like to stay with is that even before the article was written (in 1874), way back in Greek history, Hestia had the power to maintain the stability of the *foyer* which is the sacred hearth of the household and also the stability of the polis which is the political power. At that time they were combined in one. And in 1874, when this article was written, the attributes of Hestia were related to the foyer (which means the fire) and the stability of the home. It is coming back to us. All that is related to our curriculum and our profession!

Pat Thompson: Thank you. The article is a unique source. I think that people who can read it in the original French get a sense of the intensity of the idea more than we can in translation. I feel empowered by your sharing. You are confirming what my intuition told me of the relation of this idea to Home Economics.

Group Two Report

Faye: Our reading was taken from the classical dictionary and was the definition once again of Hestia, but the reference highlighted here was to Vesta, who was the Roman goddess who has the same connotation as the Greek goddess Hestia. Similar definition and similar to what we've been talking about. Then in our little group we started talking about a lot of the subjects that we teach at the high school level, and looking at some of the content and thinking about our audience. And then we went a little further and talked about the Hermean people we are always faced with.

We ended up with something you mentioned, that is, to come back with the concerns of your group and maybe some questions to go away with. One of them was this: rather than us spending a lot of time trying to convince people of what we teach and how wonderful it is and how it relates to the household and family, we would like to know how are we to politicize the process here of making the Hestian and Hermean worlds known and not necessarily to convert others to Home Economics. Where are the groups from whom we should be asking support, not necessarily from the Hermean, maybe other groups in the Hestian world, and so on. Another question we came up with and this is the last. . .We talked about the name. We looked at the definitions that refer to the family, back to the hearth goddess on high. In this particular paper, Hestia is called Vesta. We wondered what is the feeling here about name change. We discussed the number of name changes that have taken place, especially in Canada, at the secondary and postsecondary level. Name change is just a way to make you invisible!

Pat Thompson: Name change from Hestia to Vesta *is* part of the invisibility question. You find in more recent dictionaries that Hestia's name is dropped and so is Vesta's. She's not there! So this reference to Vesta in the Roman embodiment is the continuation in the next classical period of the Hestian idea. It gets progressively degraded under patriarchy. The so-called "Vestal Virgins" were important women—maybe the Home Economics teachers of their time! They were certainly the "knowledgeable women" of their time.

Group Three Report

Barbara: We also had a definition of Vesta, and it's very much as you explained it to us. We discussed fire in detail, and we recalled stories in the readers about containing the fire, carrying it to other homes. [Turning to another group member.] You should tell about your experience.

Wendy: I grew up in Northern England and a tradition on New Year's Eve was to take a live coal from your house to another person's house as a sign of good luck. This is similar to a Scandinavian tradition, which is possible because Northern England was settled by Scandinavians. I remembered that as something that had happened. And then I remembered it had to be a man who carried the fire to the house. It couldn't be a woman. It had to be a tall dark man—he had to be dark—I don't know why.

Pat Thompson: It's interesting to retrieve some of these rituals. Remember that Prometheus stole fire, probably from women. Rituals promote social bonding, even when their original *raison d'être* is forgotten. Fire remains an important element in household rituals. The next time you have a chance to see the film *Quest for Fire*, perhaps you will look at it differently.

There are many different accounts of fire rituals. I don't know if anyone had a ritual of the mother preceding her daughter in taking the fire. The point is that this is a diffused ritual. We can't get a clear account of it. As soon as things become patriarchal, ritual participation by women is gradually obscured. It is never public. It's done systematically by patriarchal gatekeepers. It's just too good for a woman to be so important in the spiritual life of humankind. So Hestia and Vesta are viewed through a male lens of analysis. This business about virgins is really funny. It's the same Old Maid idea. It's the idea that the woman who chooses to remain unmarried is somehow a reject, a second class citizen! Yet in Greek and Roman mythology when Hestia/Vesta refused to marry, she was rewarded by Zeus/Jupiter and became first among the gods to be venerated. She was the first to whom tribute was paid, and she was the last to whom tribute was paid. We still begin meals with prayer. Once they were prayers to Hestia!

In various religions we use fire in different ways. In Jewish family life, candle-lighting is the mother's ritual. It's not done by fathers. So we have several excellent things we want to recapture and pull back into our consciousness to give us a sense of the lost power of our archetypal female being. There's just no way to get away from it. At one

time Home Economics resisted being defined as a "woman's field."
Now perhaps (by turning to the Hestian metaphor) we have a tool for
our own empowerment. We can forget that we were ever ashamed of
being women or that we lost the power. Instead, it was taken from us.
Perhaps that is the essential truth of the story of Prometheus. Fire was
stolen from women! We can't allow that again, because these little
things remind us of the Hestian archetype embodied in our female
point of view on our discipline and practice.

We talk about good housekeeping. We wish our urban areas were
run like good homes. If they were, we wouldn't be spending so much
on fuel! Don't you just wish you had a big budget? We're always on the
receiving end of left-over funds, never on the priority list. The
"money men" never set money aside for Hestian education and Hestian service. That's all supposed to be done on a free basis, on a volun-
teer basis. You soon learn that if anything is Hestian, you are expected to do it for nothing. Think about what you're asked to do in society. Everything that contributes to the essential needs of human beings is supposed to be done free — for the good of your household, for
the good of your children, for the good of your husband. Romance
and love come into it! You're supposed to do all this heavy labour for
love. Shouldn't it work the other way? If women were loved, men
would spare them all this heavy effort and somehow arrange for them
to have the free time to answer important questions like "What is
morality?" "What does it mean to be a 'true woman'?" Mrs. Socrates,
Mrs. Plato, and Mrs. Aristotle would have had their ideas recorded.
Instead, they were back in the Hestian domain worrying about their
husbands' chitons, sandals, and personal habits!

Group Four Report

Paula: My group included Pat and Peggy who represents the Prince Edward Island Status of Women organization, and I teach communications. Pat chose a reading for us from the dictionary that had Hestia
and Hermes. But the new item was Hecate to whom she's referred.
Hecate is queen of the witches. She was noisy. That means she related to me and my interest in communications! Communications is
my area, and I was interested in the fact that Hecate travelled the
crossroads and people put out food to seek her out.

My research on memory tells me that you remember the first and
the last! The first issue we talked about was why do women let men
take over their leadership in a group? The last question we talked
about, when all three of us were present, centered around what are

the Hestian and Hermean versions of humour? In between we talked about what is the relationship between Home Economics and other feminist groups. Do we support each other? Do we influence each other? We have a question about how we can communicate from the Hestian group to the Hermean group. We had a comment that maybe, just maybe, we need to let the Hestian die out a little bit, not worry if it dies out, and then maybe it will come back stronger.

Pat Thompson: In ancient tradition, it was a sacrilege to let the fire die out! It meant the end of the group. Put it this way—maybe a die-back is necessary—a die-back rather than die-out. Maybe it is better for Home Economics programs that have lost their focus to go by the wayside. That way, where Home Economics continues to exist, it exists with unity of purpose. So long as our purpose is focussed, we can regroup and get other support, so long as it isn't every program, and so long as the programs that remain are genuinely focussed on the structures of everyday life and of the quality of life. We may have to face that. And we may have to accept it. So long as a spark remains, we can keep the fire burning.

Paula: We had a discussion about generalist/specialist and the relation to Hestian/Hermean; we discussed what it is we're looking for in life that will make us feel complete.

Pat Thompson: It sort of comes full circle to "What is a 'true woman'?" What does it mean to be a fulfilled female person? To characterize Hestia as an Old Maid, as some have done, is laughable. She represented human beings in the collective sense. A woman does not have to have a husband or a baby to be fulfilled. That's a myth!

Jenny: Have you read a small book where someone was relating the concept of witches? It might go back beyond this time. This person was relating it to women's healing powers and knowledge, how to use things to heal people and only God could heal, and women who had the power were very suspect, and they burned thousands and thousands of witches at the stake.

Pat Thompson: I have not read it, but actually I discovered that Hestia for me was a unifying metaphor for Home Economics. We must find out why images of women have been so debased and why heroines are only defined as opposite to heroes. There are a lot of questions that feminists are asking, and fortunately there are a lot of areas of scholarship that women are contributing to. I read a lot, but I'm not sure I can keep up with everything that is proliferating in women's scholarship. These are interesting, exciting times. My sense is that as questions arise in Home Economics we need to turn to women scholars, and ask, "What's the state of the art of Women's Studies in your discipline?" We will find out about some of the things that have been eluding us for so long. I see home economists as the intellectual quiltmakers. They're the people best able to take the bits and pieces of knowledge that other people have neglected and stitch them together into some kind of coherent, comprehensive pattern that makes sense for everyday life. It is satisfying to do this. It is art in life.

Hestian and Hermean Women's Studies

A lot of women have hold of a piece of knowledge, but they don't know what to do with it. They're stuck out there in the Hermean world, and it doesn't make any sense. They don't have anything to connect it to! We need to sit around piecing the new knowledge together. We have a curriculum built on the structures of everyday life. You can drop a lot of knowledge into that curriculum. But we don't have all the answers. Our discipline provides the receiving blanket for all this newborn knowledge!

We must not let women's scholarship go off in different directions and not be reintegrated into an improved knowledge of clothing, shelter, food, child development, and family relationships. We have to reclaim the oikos and oikonomeia through Hestian empowerment. Any Hestian knowledge that surfaces in women's scholarship is going to have to be infused into the Home Economics curriculum—or there will be no change. We can Hestianize the new scholarship in Women's Studies. We can help to bring it back into focus. When knowledge is Hermeanized, it becomes a tool of domination, not emancipation. I read in the women's literature, in Psychology, Anthropology, and Sociology. I read books here and I read books there, and I get all excited when I realize that you could spend your whole lifetime before you come to the conviction that woman the gatherer is as important as man the hunter! And there you are, you've only got one discipline. We must integrate this new scholarship.

I think that asking questions is a wonderful way to reach out to the women scholars. We should invite Women's Studies people to address our meetings. We can ask intelligent questions and build the bridges with other women scholars who don't have anybody "outside" interested in what they're doing either! You think we have a hard time being heard? I've gone to feminist education meetings where important papers were being read. And there were only three people (including me) in the audience! No men at all.

In one case, the *Sears* case in the States, you have two women historians battling it out as expert witnesses in court. They're both Hermean! We haven't been allowed to testify as Hestian experts, because to be an "expert" you must do research in a Hermean mode. Hermean language defines reality. Finally, as women scholars get to the end of their research, they say, "But what about—maybe—" because in the meantime they've gotten married, they've had children. They are aware of their households and their families. It's too late then, because they've always had their work vested in some aspect of the Hermean domain that is just a fragment of the whole. Then they try to bring it back. What we have to say is, "Hey! We're over here, and we can help you reintegrate some of your data and rephrase some of the questions that you are asking because our specialization is to integrate, to infuse meaning into diverse pieces of knowledge so that we can get it back into some kind of a meaningful whole that relates to the human condition."

Sonya: We should hold onto the core. But it seems that in many cases what is happening is that bits of the core are getting chopped off, and what is left are parts of the specializations that can be identified as belonging in the Hermean world.

Pat Thompson: That's true. Doesn't that make it clear? One square from the quilt loses the pattern of the whole. Both its beauty and its utility is destroyed if one square is taken out. Once we were talking about this question without a way to frame it. The Hestian/Hermean model helps frame it in a way that makes it clear immediately. Once we can frame the question, maybe we can organize data to support our position in a more forceful fashion. We don't have to spin our wheels quite so much. If we've said it, and we've all understood that language now, we've established a new kind of intersubjective meaning. We came to Rustico with a set of individualized concerns. We've played with some new ideas, and some new language, and if I hear you correctly, intersubjective meanings have been established.

As a community of women, we have made a change for ourselves, perhaps only ourselves now, but once you're able to establish new meaning through language, you are free to frame new questions. Maybe Home Economics can give feminism a new look. We'll understand Hestian/Hermean problems better without a lot of wasted time. It takes too much energy to argue every minor point before you can address a major question. What appear to be different problems are not different problems. They are different facets of the same problem—the Hermeanization of knowledge and of our curriculum. We must continue to deal with the Hestian aspects of food, clothing, shelter, home management, child care, and family living. So if we can define that problem, that should mean we have made progress. We can't convert those who are Hermeanized. There are some people that we're going to waste our energy on. We might better divert our energy to approach people who share our Hestian perspective.

The Hermean approach to these problems is bureaucratic. When we work in bureaucratic organizations, we are at the bottom of the organizational heap. There are a very few institutions, major institutions, where individuals who happen to be home economists are deans, college or university deans, associate deans, corporate vice-presidents, even elected public officials. As women, they sometimes have a hard time. Deans and administrators in Hermean colleges and universities are not the only people we can deal with. There are also legislators, trustees, and boards, for example. Sometimes what is happening is that because we get the message in a certain format, we respond to it in the same format in which we receive it. We get the message from a college administrator to work on name change, for example. So we run around and do what we're told. Now that we know that universally this Hermeanization of women's work (mental and physical) is taking place, forget answering. He isn't interested in what your reasons are for not changing the name. The only thing that's going to impress him is if you go outside to your legislators, trustees, alumni, to other people who are interested in Hestian education for our Home Economics curriculum. Instead of wasting energy in trying to convince Hermean administrators, build our support system through the Hestian networks, the board members, the alumni and other people. Bring pressure to bear on the institution. We must learn to use Hermean strategies for Hestian objectives!

Peggy, in our group, said, "Why is it that home economists are so passive?" I think it's true. There are a lot of passive women in Home Economics. But I can't condemn that. When a woman is passive, and she's a subject of wife abuse, women gather round and say, "How can we help this woman? Let's establish a halfway house for battered wives." But if home economists are abused, and if the profession is pressured, no one is running around saying, "Save the home economists" (save the whales!). It gives us a perspective on ourselves. Instead of looking inside, we start looking out. You take two chairs, as we do in family relations, for two sides of the argument. Now we're standing over on the Hermean side and looking at Home Economics and saying, "Well, it's all these unimportant trivial things," and we know that the voice of Home Economics isn't going to be heard individually. It has to be heard collectively, politically. And one has to get not just home economists interested: everyone has two or three friends who are free to write letters to influential people.

Paula: That's what feminists do.

Pat Thompson: Perhaps one of the things we need to learn is to stand over in the Hermean world and say, "O.K. How many votes can I get for this? How many voices can I make come out in public and yell and scream?" I don't mind yelling and screaming. Some people mind yelling and screaming. It's hard for them to do. But I can't say that they're deficient because they don't care to be vocal. Sometimes, when your profession's life is on the line, that's what you have to do. It's important enough to get out and become a vocal person. But you're also glad to have leaders in the right places who can give you clear, unambiguous messages about the danger that may be imminent. I find, and I'm sure you do too, too many people, who work in the field and gain their livelihood from the field, who have no idea what is going on in it. And that is appalling. Women actually collude in their own destruction. Sometimes, we are our own worst enemy!

Group Five Report

Pat Thompson: Any other thoughts? Let's turn to Ward Shipman's brief use of this Hestian idea in the *Family Analysis Handbook*. I came upon this paragraph after developing my arguments, as I was thumbing through a book in a friend's library a week ago, and it just hit me. I said, "What's Hestia doing in this book?" And I found this notion that "Hestia" might be an adjective applied to family climate. How do you respond to that?

Ellie: I think there are a lot of fads in social sciences and in other areas as well. They get a new term and they run it to death. I wonder if this is an idea that will be picked up and will be debased and misused. It didn't seem to me that it was used in the sense at all that you're using it.

Pat Thompson: I think it may be the other way. That he doesn't really understand what Hestia symbolized from a genuine feminist perspective. He had the idea, but he didn't know where to go with it. It's these bits of references that you read, these fragments and how they fit with something that you already knew and already had experienced, and already had thought about that is so exciting. I think this sort of floated around the surface of his thinking. But I was startled that somebody had even gotten that close.

Ellie: That's what I'm afraid of. That somebody would grab the idea from reading that and run off with it without a full understanding, and perhaps damage any views we might take of it. We can't copyright the term. But sometimes a term is used and it's perfectly good, but it gets debased through misuse.

Pat Thompson: That's true — there could be a debasement of the term Hestian. That's not the subject of my research, so I can't say. Women work a lot through intuition, and I'm not ashamed to work along intuitive lines because certainly my grasp of Hestia and your grasp of Hestia is intuitive. You're getting it from fragments, but you're saying that those fragments fit with some frameworks that I have sketched. You're not finding this so alien, so foreign, so awkward that you say, "I can't fit this into my thought patterns." So I think we are justified, maybe because we are women, to go on "women's intuition." Yea for women's intuition! There are always things that can't be made explicit. People want everything made explicit. Nobody's going to live long enough to meet these demands. So we must make some demands of our own.

Do you ever wonder that you stay in Home Economics? What is this hold that Home Economics has on you? I guess that sounds disloyal, but you know you really have to look at it and say, "Some of this is awfully strange. No wonder people misunderstand."

Trudi: I don't think it's disloyal. Certainly some Home Economics graduates don't have a sense of Home Economics as a field. They don't themselves seem to see that it integrates all of these things. They would probably say, "I took Home Economics because I wanted to learn to cook and sew, or I wanted to get married later and I thought that would be a good background." I think that's probably still so. That's my impression sometimes.

Pat Thompson: Is it so wrong to have a Hestian vocation? Even if people don't articulate it as such, homemaking is a Hestian vocation. It is, after all, real work. Hermeans can't have a monopoly on everything! As one who doesn't have an undergraduate background in Home Economics, and who came to it so much later in life, let me ask you as a collectivity of women — what about women's life course and our maturing as part of our awareness of the field's significance? Is it something that we fully grasp as young women at 16 or 18? No! It comes to us with greatest force later in life. We may enjoy what we're doing, but intellectually is it something we can see as quickly and as immediately as people are able to see the relevance of Hermean disciplines?

Faye: That's something we did discuss in our group, about the curriculum. We brought it down to the junior high and senior high levels. If you look at the adolescent at that particular age, their family doesn't have the same meaning to them at that age as later in life. So how do we make that relevant for them?

Pat Thompson: And in a contemporary society that allows you to scoot off and get pregnant and come back with new babies, babies having babies, fourteen-year-olds and even younger having babies, and sometimes coming back to their parents' homes and sometimes leaving their children for other people to care for. That's very fortunate for people who choose to adopt, but many of the children who are left, for one or another reason, are not adoptable. And that makes a bereft generation of children who are neglected and whose prognosis is dismal.

I think of the women—and men—who came together at Lake Placid at the turn of the century as mature people. They were people who had lived a life. And Ellen Richards had lived a whole life as a scientist and an academic. And Home Economics was her "mature" vision. It wasn't something she dreamed up as a young woman. One of my young colleagues—Cathy Daly at the University of Minnesota—did research in Anthropology and in textiles and clothing among the Kalabari women of Western Nigeria. She was interested in the way women communicate coming of age through the symbolism of clothing—coming of age and changing status for women. And she said, "This is communicated through the knowledgeable women of the tribe." I love that phrase "knowledgeable women," because it means that women who have processed a lot of information and are well-respected in the tribe are turned to as the repositories of the tribe's wisdom for women. Our feminist colleagues joke about "experts on housework." There's a big difference between categorizing and diminishing our contributions as experts on housework and being knowledgeable women. I said, "Cathy, what a wonderful concept of what Home Economics is. Did you ever think that these knowledgeable women in the Kalabari tribe are the home economists of the Kalabari? They've got the whole picture from birth to death. Everything a woman needs to function and operate intelligently in her culture." So I began to wonder about Home Economics. We're trying to deal with young women and wondering why we can't perhaps attract younger women? Maybe it is because our maturity helps us to see these things. After all, when I was younger I thought Home Economics meant cooking and sewing. It took me a long time to learn that this was a very superficial view. But in a society that doesn't value maturity for women don't we become the stereotype?

Faye: Name changes—and a fragmentation—because Home Economics tried to make an inroad and it's impossible, so our young people can't relate to this mature profession!

Pat Thompson: Yes. Not only do we have to confront the fact that we are in a female-defined discipline, and that women are generally de-valued, but here we are. I guess young Heather is the very youngest in the group right now. How old are you Heather? Twenty! From twenty to sixty and all the ages in between—O.K. retirees—but I think it's important for women to deal with their age. It was easy when I was forty-five—I could say "I'm forty-five!" But every year it got harder and when I hit fifty-five—am I going to be able to say sixty? And I thought, as I thought when I was younger, that to lie about one's age was a really desperate thing for women to do. So here I am at sixty—looking back at my life course from twenty to thirty, and thirty to forty, and forty to fifty, and fifty to sixty. And thinking of that, what does that represent? And of course I think of the women who founded this discipline, and I realize that most of them were probably in their late forties or older. They had lived a rich professional life.

Paula: Well maybe not quite. Alice Ravenhill wouldn't be that old.

Pat Thompson: What do you mean, "that old!"

Paula: She might have been in her late thirties.

Pat Thompson: O.K. But in those days still a candidate for old bagship. She never married did she?

Paula: No.

Pat Thompson: "Old maidship", then! A reject! Who wants to hear from a woman who has no man to validate her! Ninety-five years old and never married! What could she have to tell us? Anyhow, it's something we have to consider. Is this one of the great benefits of being mature women—that we can look at certain issues from the per-spective of the woman's life course and integrate that? It seems to me that the founders of Home Economics were looking back and speak-ing out of the culmination of their own wisdom, of their lives lived. They looked at what had been necessary and what had been lacking, and then they tried to formulate all that into a curriculum. They knew what was ahead in life! They wanted women to be prepared—to empower them!

Faye: That's interesting. I had read that there is some thought whether Home Economics should be a school subject or a course more relevant to adults.

Pat Thompson: It does depend on one's perspective. From my perspective, I think we want to get students from the very beginning—just as the Vestals got the little girls at ten, and you might get both the little girls and the little boys at ten before they get to be fathers and mothers, so that they have some participatory learning about what the life course holds. Maybe we can head them off at the pass before they become teenage parents.

Faye: Yes. But if the solution to that is to follow through with some of the decision-makers in the Hermean sphere, rather than call it Home Economics, give it a new name like "independence skills," "living on your own," you know, that format.

Pat Thompson: I think it's perfectly legitimate to call a curriculum or a course anything you want in order to get the kids interested. The danger is in abandoning the identity of the discipline and the academic units with respect to the discipline. There are people who don't agree with me that Home Economics is a discipline. But I believe Home Economics is the discipline of everyday life. Its knowledge is organized around the structures, the immutable perennial problems, of everyday life. It may look different from another discipline, but it is rigorous because it includes certain things and excludes others. There are some things that are highly relevant and other things that are less relevant. But from the systems perspective, the remotest thing which ultimately has relevance for the Hestian domain must be considered part of the discipline and of the curriculum.

When we make decisions concerning what is relevant, we have to make them based on Hestian thinking without being bent out of shape by Hermean thinkers! In the early days it came spontaneously from the women who made decisions, and they were accepted by the administrators in the different universities. Now we're playing a different game. We're finding an increasingly Hermeanized public world in which there's a great deal to be gained by the Hermean world if we fail.

Somehow we have to deal with all the misfits and all the divorces, and all the messed up lives, to be fixed up later by public agencies! You can only patch them up. You can't really make them whole as you could if you got in early.

In a sense, as mothers and fathers leave the Hestian domain with less influence on their children, it becomes more important to reach children early than to put time and energy into the response to some curricular description. Changes in the Hestian domain make it more necessary to make decisions. Instead of arguing for learning later in adult life, when the mistakes have been made, schools have to educate for everyday life from kindergarten on. Day care! Now if we can contribute to day care education—the hand that rocks the cradle rules the world! If we could get back to that cradle-rocking and remain the shapers of children, ages two-and-a-half to five we would change the world. There would be no question—if we had the greatest influence on that level of education—pre-K, kindergarten, first grade. That's where Hestian education is important because it's important in terms of the child's self-image. Children must learn how to care for themselves in terms of their elemental everyday needs. If their families can't attend to that, then we need to take care of that in the school. But people's questions are Hermean. Their solutions are Hermean. Day care is becoming "Big Business." What does that have to do with children's ability to live or to earn a living? How can people earn a living if they are personally disorganized and psychologically off-base? The "Big Business"—franchised day care—is ludicrous. It shows how limited the Hermean view of education is. Because if you don't have a whole person to employ, where are you?

Trudi: I offer another thought on the name "Home Economics" for junior and senior high school. I can see some advantages to not calling courses "Home Economics" because people will say, "We took Home Economics in high school and we know what it's all about."

Maureen: I'm afraid if we have all these different names, no one will have a concept of what Home Economics is. When I started teaching my grade 8s, I felt frustrated that they came in with such a negative image of Home Economics. And after the first year I always started the first day by asking them what their impression was. And then I'd say, "What do you see as being essential to your survival? Open your books and list whatever number of things you can think of." And always there'd be one or two who would say money, jobs. But they always would say food, shelter, and once you give them a hint, clothing. They'd say something about child care and so on. And we'd get the five essentials and maybe a few tangential things and then I'd say, "Now what do you need to be able to supply these things?" They'd soon start to see where everything goes together.

Pat Thompson: Can any other discipline start from that perspective?

Maureen: No, I doubt it. I have to tell you this because it was so heart warming. I had a male student. His mother was a home economist, and he came home the first day of school after his class—the only time I had any feedback on this—and she said, "Carl came home today and said, 'We did nothing in any of the classes except Home Economics. And you know, there's a lot more to Home Economics than I ever thought there was'." And that just reinforced me so much. So if you tell them (even if they're not mature) they *can* see the whole. Then later on they'll put more pieces into it.

Pat Thompson: You've just elaborated the Hestian perspective. You delineated those things that are essential to survival. Most people (unless they are totally distorted and spoiled) can recognize that there are some things that are essential to survival that everyone must learn. Then we go beyond survival to improve the quality of life. The next level is to ask what knowledge you might need to add quality—ethics and aesthetics—to these five or six issues that you delineated. If people will just get back to that, to the notion of the essentials, and let people dwell on that long enough, they do come up with the right answer!

Wendy: They do know it. They know that they need it. But they are still facing this Hermean side. All their values and all the influences that are saying, "But I need to get a job"—or whatever. But I know they see that part of it.

Pat Thompson: I don't want to denigrate the Hermean world because we do live in it. We function by those norms. But to forget the Hestian does terrible disservice to the well-rounded human being. It ignores the question of the quality of life. So by approaching it the way you do, this seems to me that that's it.

Chris: In Nova Scotia in social studies right now they're pushing the family aspect to try to make courses more relevant. Industrial arts (which has always been very technologically based) now has a family focus in their most recent statement.

Pat Thompson: How to make fire!

Chris: Looking more from a family point of view.

Pat Thompson: Who's trained for it? Industrial arts teachers are not trained to teach the family! That's the real question.

Ellie: Frightening. . .

Pat Thompson: Yes, frightening in some respects, but not if you are anticipating this and collectively reinforcing yourselves to claim your territory as the Hestian territory. What they're doing is chipping it away, and you're saying, "How do I fight this battle on their terms?" I say move it to the territory where you're knowledgeable, where you are the knowledgeable women. That kind of empowerment could change the game. We must change the game, not the name! It doesn't have to be every one of you, but each of you becoming empowered differently from the Hestian perspective could select the people who are the most verbal or articulate for the Hermean world. We have formulated this perspective collectively and maybe we don't all articulate it, maybe back home there are a few women who aren't totally convinced, but still want to hold onto their jobs. But those persons who are most articulate are the ones that need your support. Women are not used to supporting women leaders. We're not used to saying, "That woman speaks for us." They defer to men. They want men to speak for them! Feminists have done a wonderful job in getting some media type feminists who do a very good job. The reason they have is that behind them are dozens of women who say, "She speaks for me." Home economists need to do that.

Kathy: A few weeks ago in Newfoundland there was a program on the 6:30 news about the nutritional status of Newfoundland children. Health and Welfare had done a study that was presented from a health perspective. And our special interest council might get together and do some kind of news thing afterwards. But I think they do cover nutrition and health. I think the more areas they do touch on the information the more valid it is in the eyes of the students. No matter if they cover something on nutrition in science or health or whatever, they still have to see us as the integrating unit and the practical application. And we don't get that anywhere else, and we have to make sure they see that.

Pat Thompson: Ideally they will see the relationship, but if singling out one aspect of the total picture is made to appear to be the whole, we see it as people saying, "Nutrition! I can understand that. That's specific. Our kids should know nutrition. We want them well fed." From the perspective of curriculum theory, there are a lot of questions to ask. Why are you assuming perhaps that poor nutrition is a function of poverty? Poor nutrition isn't a function of poverty; in many cases poor kids eat better than rich kids. So that's the first thing that people have to understand. How do we separate nutrition from family resource management? It really can't be done! Family formation, family management, family decision-making! A hundred things are relevant because they are interrelated—the equipment in the family, the Hestian space, the community, a lot of things. Then they say, "But I didn't realize all these are related," and you say, "Yes they are!"

Sandra: There's another piece of information that has been made public. Kids in grade 4 and grade 7 across the country don't sleep at night. There's a connection to be made between what happens at home and what happens in the wider world. And the response, the solution that was proposed, was that these kids have to be psychologically helped by a professional to sleep! But my humble opinion is that the world is a darn scary place for kids, and they know that the future of the world is at stake. They see enough television. They hear enough of what's going on, Star Wars and other things that are in the high technological area, and they sense the possibilities of totally destroying the world. Without any research to back me up, I would say that they need to put the emphasis on why kids are scared. Kids need reassurance at home, from caring families who understand their fears.

Pat Thompson: Nobody wants to say that in order to hold the attention of the adult viewer, we intensify responses and we make them violent. I don't have any small children at home, and when I'm writing something and I watch these special effects, I find it's just madness—magic in a way. But if I were a seven-year-old—I had enough sorrow in my life when I was a little girl. It's bad to be beaten. It hurts. And it does something to your self-esteem, I can assure you. I can remember the mass media, the vivid impressions of "crime stories" that were featured in the Sunday rags, the papers.

For some of these things to be remedied, adults have to take time with children. Are parents going to find that time? If not parents, who? Where are we going to find the adults if it isn't parents, and by "parents" we usually mean mothers. We're right back to square one!

Sandra: But essentially that fits in with the integrated approach to wholesome living. And that's the area Home Economics has to deal with.

Pat Thompson: I wonder if we deal with it in that sense?

Sandra: We probably don't, but it fits there. It's something I think we need to get a handle on, because if that's the way kids are going to bed at night, you wonder what their grown-up life is going to be like.

Pat Thompson: Maybe they'll transcend it, and maybe they won't. And that's what worries me. They could keep the wakeful nights, going to bed fearful for the next generation.

Sandra: And going to bed hungry.

Pat Thompson: I'm certain that disproportionate numbers of children go to bed hungry, cold, and lonely. Home economists should think about these things and think about becoming spokespersons for these issues. Not every one of us has to be one, but what we have to do is give our support to those who can communicate the Hestian message effectively to the Hermean world. It's difficult. We sometimes get locked into a kind of defensiveness as women that is self-destructive. I hate to say it, but I think sometimes we get envious and jealous of other women and their kids. But we have to have consciousness-raising to become a collectivity. We have to do what the feminists do and that is learn to trust one another as a sisterhood. I think of other home economists as a sisterhood. I don't think of them just as other professionals. I'm able to count on a particular Hestian perspective, not particular qualities that a home economist has, but a perspective. In my heart of hearts I sense it as a Hestian sisterhood. I would place a lot of confidence in the ultimate value system of someone that I know is making a commitment to Home Economics — not just having a job in Home Economics, someone who is making a day-by-day commitment to Home Economics as a vehicle by which to improve individual, family, and community living. Because it's Hestian, that's what I value. That's what I believe is important. That's what I've chosen to focus on!

I'm pleased that so many of you are so thoughtful and so reflective. We have to have the time to think. We have to have the time to be intellectual. Otherwise, we're going to be caught up in old thought patterns and never have the chance to re-examine our professional lives. We can't do that for very long and survive. We need to do it the way women used to have quilting bees. We need to have thinking bees, so that your idea and my idea, and your interpretation of this reading and mine on that reading, and your experience in this and mine in that are connected. That's how knowledgeable women of the past kept it going. Not through some monumental pieces of research, but through testing out ideas with one another on an informal basis, then moving around and saying, "That works for me. I face the same problems. If it works for other women, maybe it will work for me and the women that I deal with or the families that I deal with." We shouldn't be intimidated by the fact that our Hestian mode is different from the

Hermean mode. But we can't let it destroy us. We can't let it be forgotten that the way the fire was lit the first time was through the concentration of rays from the sun, or through friction of two sticks. It's very simple. But we must control technology for a Hestian purpose, for the unity of purpose, of a higher quality of life for the next generation. It isn't a question of consuming everything in this generation and to heck with everything after that. The least we can do is leave society a trifle better than it was when we came into it. And that's not something that's fashionable to talk about.

Maureen: Could I suggest to you that we formulate or plan another reflective weekend or something in the States, and we come down and go to a spa somewhere or something? We just don't do that as home economists!

Pat Thompson: Let me suggest that you join the Home Economics Research Special Interest Group of the American Educational Research Association. It's a new network for keeping people informed about research and theory in Home Economics education at every level.

It really is important for us to maintain a transnational communication network. Because anything that can contribute to reinforcing us is something that we need to do as a Hestian collectivity. For example, let's talk about informal research. When I hear that, not only in the United States but in Canada, home economists face the problem of name change and administrative recognition, that's empirical evidence of the universality of the problem. I have to say, "Look, this is not us. This is patriarchy." Something is being done to us! No group of women can work so hard with such dedicated action towards such significant aims and be frustrated here, there and everywhere. Some larger structural force is weighing down on us, working against us. We don't have the opportunity to authentically legitimate our Hestian vision. We can work on that, once we know what the problem is. I say it is Hermean hegemony. Patriarchy! We can be energized. But not in the conventional way. We're not going to win if we get drawn into the Hermean territory to fight the battle on Hermean terms alone. We need a kind of flanking strategy, where we find out where our supports are outside the Hestian system. We've got to understand that. We've got to recognize it. And we've got to put a stop to the Hermean rape of our Hestian discipline! We've got to put a stop to it. Because it's been reported over and over again. The man comes in, makes the decisions, and women then subordinate their projects to fall into line, because they think he's going to protect them. But what does he do? He flaps his wings and says, "I'm off to a higher job and I don't care what happens to your unit or your administrative work." It is not that males are male. It is not our husbands or our lovers or our sons that are the enemy. It is patriarchy. It is the assumption that male privilege is justified. Even for mediocre men! The men who have ambitions, who are not our husbands, our lovers, or friends, don't owe us anything. They benefit from patriarchy. And it's a mistake for women to transfer their loyalty to a Hermean system that doesn't have Hestian interests at stake. That's a lot different from arguing that patriarchy needs to be replaced by matriarchy. The drive to dominate and control is Hermean. The desire to connect and collaborate is Hestian. We need a Hestian manifesto!

We have some volunteers here among these French-speaking home economists to take some of the French primary sources and look at them from the standpoint of Home Economics. It's not so difficult to find someone to translate material. It's very hard to find a set of eyes who can read texts in a second language and see them in the context of Home Economics. We are going to have some very important input from our French group, because the intellectual line of development on Hestia seems to me to have been in France. The classic work is by Jean-Pierre Vernant. Scholars took ideas from Vernant. But Martin came before that! They are all in a line, and they all deal with this Hestian/Hermean notion, but of course from the point of view of different disciplines. So for us to become prepared to retrieve and reinterpret the source materials, primary sources, from the perspective of an individual who is *au courant* in both Home Economics and in French creates a great resource for us. And it means, I think, that we will be able to cut off a good ten years of research time.

The diffusion of new ideas is very time consuming. And do you know who the last people are to get them? We are. Because no one assumes that we are going to be interested in anything. If we initiate, originate, and lay claim to new ideas, then my notion is that that is *our* intellectual territory. Other scholars then have to say, cite, and give recognition to the fact that these ideas have been developed in the discipline of Home Economics. That is my personal agenda.

Here's what I mean by that. When an idea is articulated, and if it is found to have intellectual value, it should be identified not so much with Pat Thompson but with the discipline of Home Economics. I'll live and die, but Home Economics has to live and it has to go on from the past to the present and to the future. And it's really only our scholarship and our teaching and our philosophical discussions that can reanimate Home Economics for the future. We must rekindle the fire. We can do this. We have been revaluating some of our positions, some of our points of view, and then we've been synthesizing, each of us coming from a different perspective. So many new pieces have been stitched into the quilt, so to speak. They're beginning to take shape, and we have to reflect on them. In the last couple of years with these ideas, everything is coming into focus for me. It's more than one person can do; it's something that many people have to contribute to, if it has validity and if it is going to contribute to the ongoing vitality of our field.

DIVERTISSEMENT

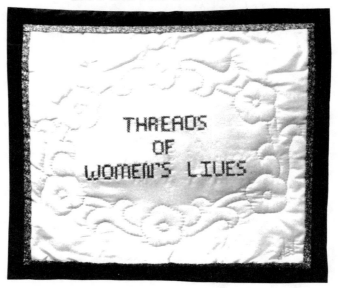

Quilts symbolize women's ways of stitching together the many facets of their lives and experience. The adaptation of the musical play *Quilters* was pieced together from a display of local quilts (one of which was quilted by a Hestian male), readings by a local reader, slides of Prince Edward Island quilts from Confederation Centre in Charlottetown, and a specially prepared audio tape of music and readings from the play. Its portrayal of the experience of pioneer women expressed through quilts and quilting was particularly effective in the setting of Belcourt Centre.

The event of the workshop which was titled "Divertissement" has since been developed into an audio-visual program and has been renamed "Threads of Women's Lives". It is available for group presentation from the Department of Home Economics, U.P.E.I.

4

EMPOWERING OUR HESTIAN PROFESSION

To begin to differentiate between public and private spheres requires, minimally, a shared language and tradition and human subjects sophisticated enough to orient themselves in the world through categories of thought which allow for comparisons, contrasts, and the establishment of relationships between one thing and another.

Jean Bethke Elshtain
Public Man, Private Woman.

FOR NOW, as we plan to leave, I want each of you to take a moment to meditate on your experiences here in Rustico and write in individual form what new ideas of whatever sort, not just from myself, but from your discussions with your colleagues, and from the wonderful *"divertissement"* we had last night. Record a few fresh or new ideas. I'm not asking for an evaluation of their utility, but whether they work for you personally. And then after you've written one idea independently, I'm going to ask that you get into different groups of three and then write a group statement of where we might go from here as a professional collective. So that we'll have some sharing and that we have some sense of moving forward, not just questions or applications, but how intellectually we ought to begin to go into the world with whatever is new and fresh for us so that we may help in the transformation process.

Barbara: Personal and professional growth go hand in hand. I have a little trouble with the professional part. I still have to scrub my kitchen counter before I leave, because I feel guilty seeing it messy like that if I'm a home economist. Of course, I'm from the old school! I also cannot tolerate coming back home to the untidy counter. I'd rather get up 20 minutes earlier so that I can have it tidy. Maybe if I was really committed to the profession, I'd leave it. But I can only tolerate so much!

Pat Thompson: You're an order-making creature. That's counter-entropic. You have a right to that Hestian order-making feeling. It's archetypal!

Barbara: I understand that, because I can't handle it if it's not tidy.

Pat Thompson: Not all of us have the same need for order in the same way. Sometimes we have perhaps projected through home management the need for everyone to have the same standard of order. I'm interested in the order in the universe, let alone my kitchen! So I just want you all to tap into Barbara's statement on ordering. That's a Hestian characteristic and quality: the need to order space, the need to keep the near environment in a way in which you can freely and best function. Valuing the ways in which you can freely and best function is different for different people and families. But the order-making process is universal. We don't have to feel guilty. When we talk with other women's groups now, we will be able to bring into their consciousness that many of them also have an order-making need. That's where we as professionals have a great deal to contribute. Because those needs have never been identified in the Hermean world as significant for personal growth and development and peace of mind. We're entitled to peace of mind. I'm glad you brought that in.

Gail: Professionally you can't present one set of values and then privately not follow through. Your professional and your personal life have to be in sync (whatever that is), and you're just defeating yourself and dividing yourself if professionally you say one thing and privately you do something else. That can't work for you.

Pat Thompson: You're saying that being an integrated person and being part of an integrated profession are congruent. And I think that's true. We have to be able to tell people that the congruence we are seeking in the Hestian domain is the congruence between individual integration and intellectual integration and the ordering of our environment and our everyday life in ways that make ethical and aesthetic sense.

Debbie: We talked quite a bit, and I found myself trying to keep up with the conversation and trying to get it down on paper. We felt that the idea of the Hestian domain is a very challenging one to home economists. Our students will be quite excited about it because we're excited about it. It provides a wonderful metaphor for what we do. It puts the wide boundaries of our discipline and the breadth of our knowledge into focus. We believe that learning more about this and being able to articulate it should make it easier in our communications with others to explain the discipline and to deal with the essentials. We think our communications with others must begin with home economists so that they see the boundaries of our field, and this might help us to explain to students why they take Psychology and Sociology and Chemistry and that they have to put it together in a unified whole.

Pat Thompson: Hearing you say that reinforces my commitment.

Debbie: We got into the challenge of communicating the Hestian idea, improving the visibility of Home Economics in the community, keeping this workshop in the back of our minds. We can see it being difficult. We thought maybe Canadian Home Economics Association should set up a task force to explore further these ideas that you have enunciated, in terms of its meaning to the profession in Canada. And that communicating on a local level is something that small associations should work on because we have to give meaning to the profession as we explain it to others. Our members have to know about it, and perhaps community groups and related professional groups as well. We considered nurses, health educators, teachers, social workers, other professionals in the community who are sort of using bits of our knowledge, bits of our field, but not pulling in the whole and making an integrated unit of it. We talked a little bit about whether we work along with them or whether they are our competitors, but we thought perhaps there could be better understanding of where we fit into the professional field—where our discipline fits into the knowledge base. It fits in, of course, in our view as basic, the most basic there is. We hope we will continue working on this idea and that it not disappear from view once we say goodbye to each other.

Pat Thompson: You have identified some other groups and professions with a Hestian orientation. I think teaching, nursing, and social work are also Hestian!

Debbie: We thought we each needed more time to reflect and to think about it and our own personal understanding of what it was. The question that we asked was, how would the contact be maintained in a uniform way? If we all go off into different parts of the country and formulate our concepts, will they also have to be slightly different? From that we thought that maybe we need a good solid body of knowledge to draw from that would be available to all of us, and that perhaps articles could be written based on the tapes that would be edited including the mailing list of those of us who are here. It was also thought that it could be used as a theoretical framework for home economists doing research and that through conversations with other people in universities on a one-to-one basis it would become known in our discipline and also in disciplines that we work with because we are so interdisciplinary.

Sandra: We had three different starting points in the three presentations in our group. I have a summary of our sense of what was happening. We agreed on the things that each person said, so this is a summary of our statements. We value a new language to use to explain Home Economics. The intellectual stimulus of this session was great. There was a sense of starting down a new road. Although travelled before, there was a newness about it and a sense of adventure with regard to Home Economics. The Hestian outlook is a new outlook not only on Home Economics, but on everyday living experience. It reinforces beliefs and gives new life and courage to do and to communicate. Education in equality between the Hestian and the Hermean domains needs to be done at all grade levels, at all ages. In our professional communication we can reclaim, reaffirm, revalue the symbols of Home Economics, and interpret this to others, and through them hopefully gain respect for our values and our goals and our aims which are all-encompassing of human life, past, present and future.

All of us expressed a new excitement, a new fire, a new experience of the value of Home Economics. New life has been infused into us regarding our profession. I have one reflection that came out of a couple of comments that were made today and in the last few days. As a group of professionals we are inclined to be apologetic (like battered women), but people don't know about us; we are not very good at communicating. I really think we have to be very careful that we don't blame ourselves. Then people will better understand and appreciate what we're about.

Debbie: We try to communicate more with the Hermeans in a sense. Maybe we should change that.

Sandra: I agree with what has been presented already, that we ought to start communicating among the Hestians and with other women's groups. The women's publications I think are important for us to get at, and we'll probably have some minds there that are open.

There's one other point that I'd like to add. I really feel very strongly about communicating our symbols. Symbolism is a very, very strong method of communication: fire for instance, as a symbol;

Hestia as a symbol; needle and thread as a symbol. It's reclaiming and revaluing how they fit in the total long view, past, present, and future, and extension outward into the areas of human life and the quality of life. What does that mean? It means that we put together things, using the broader example putting together fabric to make a garment or a quilt or whatever. But to use it as a symbol—to go further, to explain this. I have a new appreciation after this workshop—needle and thread—cradle—things like that we really need to say—they are important, they are valuable.

Kathy: In my group we came up with many things that are already mentioned. First of all we thought it's very important to explain to other home economists the information we have received. We published a copy of your article in the *Illinois Teacher* in our local newsletter, and people were truly astounded. They said, "What's it all about?" They shook their heads and put it to one side. I didn't fully understand it myself. I think that we need to go back and talk about it with our groups. A lot of people are very confused about it. We obviously are not as in tune with it as you are, but at least we are on the road there to help people understand this concept. So we must explain to home economists why our work is considered invisible, and stop blaming ourselves. As you mentioned, we have done this too much: our fault, our image, our this, our that. And this would help us to develop a better self-esteem and stop putting ourselves down. We had a Home Economics student in our group, and I think that's maybe why we should mention that—there's just one Home Economics student here, a university student—and if we can communicate this to students, it will give them a better feeling about what it is to be a home economist. You mentioned about feeling inferior very often to the other subject areas. It would help young Home Economics students to feel better about what it is to be a home economist.

We also talked about how to communicate with the general public, how to try to be more visible, what did we get intellectually, supporting one another, and more openness. We talked about how hard it is to be Home Economics teachers. Very often we work on our own. We don't talk about what we do. We may share things in our own departments, but we don't share very much with other departments. And I think one thing that came out of this for me in my group is the need to open up more, to talk about what we do and to use the metaphor to explain who we are and the importance of our work to our administrators. We continually defend what we do to fight against program cuts and things like that, and this will be a useful way of trying to explain why we have to be there.

Lastly, we talked about how to help other groups of women who are struggling with other problems. In my area, for example, battered women have been struggling for years to get a house for battered women, to get a shelter, and this is part of their struggle. They were dealing with the Hermean world—politics oh politics—and that seems to be an easy way to explain the problem. But I think there's a deeper meaning; deeper than politics. We could help. We could give these thoughts to other women's groups who are dealing with many problems related to women and families.

Pat Thompson: Consider this. Politics is the Hermean mode. Home Economics is the Hestian mode. They apply to two different spheres of human action.

Paula: We're a small group. We used our time to clarify our thinking. We felt that our problem was to apply what we've been talking about, learning about Hestia, to our own situation when we return to our own location. Our short pieces are personal. Both of us expressed concern about the state of our profession at the moment. We wanted to look for positives, since we were feeling depressed, and the positive thing is that we found that we are all feeling the same thing. Therefore, we should get together and go on and make changes. Maureen works with junior high school people so she has decided that her contribution will be to help the students understand what Home Economics is. I'm at the University level, so I want to tell my students, also, and apply these ideas in the research area. Since I'm in communications, maybe I can do something about the study of language which is the point that Pat has been making.

We also felt concern about what feminists think about Home Economics. Again we felt that there were a lot of negative thoughts being expressed, and we wanted to see how we can help feminists understand Home Economics better.

Maureen: I am definitely a feminist, and when I was talking about conflict I was thinking about when you're in with feminists, none of whom are home economists, who remember little tidbits of Home Economics classes that they have interpreted in a negative way. They were acquired at different times, but from their point of view we are still back there in that time. History is what we studied in Grade 9, I suppose. Yet history has changed in school. I don't know that we really appreciate that. And they probably don't see—they can't see—the changes in our profession. So when we say things that make feminists sound like some enemy group sometimes, I don't think we want it to sound that way. I don't think that's what it is. But this has helped me to resolve the conflict to a certain degree. The conflict I realize now has come from this other sphere that evaluated the profession from a certain point of view, that has demeaned certain Home Economics values. And I think I do feel a little better equipped to respond when things come up and I think we need to be—Paula was talking about being a communicator, and I've been involved in public speaking, and I think there's always a chance for us to offer to speak to Women's Institutes, to speak to sororities, to speak everywhere where there are women's groups, because they will understand our language better, and they all have somebody in their life that they can pass it on to.

Susan: I think that what feminists usually think when they think of home economists is this—and in this they are similar to many minority people. When I first started teaching there were parents in Black and Spanish groups who did not want their daughters at that time to take Home Economics because they didn't want them to be servants. And I think this is still the feminist concept of what we do: that we are developing women who serve other people, right down to making coffee in the office. Their original objection, for example, to having men in feminist circles was that, if the men come in, we'll be making coffee for them and they'll be doing all the decision-making. And I think what we have to try to get across to them, whether we invite ourselves to their meetings or invite them to ours or submit articles to their journals, is that we are developing people, not developing people to serve other people. It's a very hard thing to break through this stereotype that we're not creating servants, we're creating people who can help themselves as well as anybody else.

Faye: Another thing that we could bring to our feminist groups—I myself am involved—and one thing that became very clear to me was that they are very concerned about helping other women to be more assertive and able to look after themselves. However, they never thought of our profession, and I don't think we made that clear to them—I know I didn't at the time. I'm certainly thinking about it now, and this two-day conference has given me more ammunition and made me feel better able to cope with that whole situation—that we deal with women. Our audience is female. And I mean, here they are going out saying we want you and let's get help from the Government to get these grants to have workshops. Well, here we are with these young women in our classes who are at this very influential stage of their life. Why aren't they coming to us and working with us and all of us working together to educate and make these young women better human beings, better able to cope with all the conflicts and the turmoil in the Hermean world that they will be confronted with? Where I do a lot of thinking is about presenting the Hestian/Hermean concept to them, but at the same time have them think of our potential and how much we can add to that whole.

Home Economists As Hestian Feminists

What Faye just said was the wrap-up idea. Is a Home Economics/ Feminist synthesis possible? That's the question you're asking. I want to thank you so for your reports. They are wonderful! I'd like now to return to the language of Dean Drake. I think it's a good thing to conclude with the notion of "unity of purpose." I think it was wonderful that he used that language when he introduced the conference, and I think it's a good thing for us to return to it now with your ideas, synthesizing, syn-cretizing, and synergizing with one another.

Had I not been a feminist, I could not have come to this greater under-standing of Home Economics. Home Economics is a discipline that we have to look at objectively from a feminist perspective. We can see it as a disadvantaged profession for reasons many of you have said are not to be found in the individual profession but are found in the forces of the soci-ety that depreciates everything related to being female and to the Hes-tian outlook on the world. Feminists do not have a monopoly on women's issues, and somehow through the past decades, Home Economics has had the worst of it. Every bit of anguish and anger that feminists have felt about their role and status as women has been pro-jected onto Home Economics uncritically. And some home economists, understandably, have internalized this. However, the fact that Home Economics survived this kind of disdain from women and from the Hermean world is to me a testimony to the fact that there is something so vital, so essential, so humanly imperative about Home Economics that we are now at a point where we can break out of this containment and begin to do some of the things that you have talked about. This means to build bridges, primarily to other women's groups in a context that they can accept. Now what I think will be a surprise to feminists is that home economists really have a foundation and a con-ceptual framework into which many of their ideas fit. You know most of us are teachers, and we know the naiveté of the newcomer. And for feminists who have come upon a problem for the first time, everything is new and, truthfully, one looks at their behaviour and activities as essen-tially naive because there is no sophisticated history behind all this. The history of suffrage is not the history of women. Suffrage was a Hermean women's movement. Home Economics was a Hestian women's move-ment. Women's problems do not begin or end with suffrage, but they will begin and end with the essential problems of everyday life—the perennial problems of daily living that women seem uniquely concerned about.

We've come full circle from a beginning to an end, and become contained in the concept and the values of the Hestian domain in our thinking. From this point we might think about whether we are Hestian feminists. There is no word for the kind of feminists home economists are, because to be a feminist sometimes has an alien sound. It sounds as though we want only to get into the Hermean world. I think the mainstreams of feminism (Marxist Feminism, Liberal Feminism, Socialist Feminism, and Radical Feminism) are largely Hermean women's movements. They often emulate what males do and advocate male norms and male strategies for women as though those norms and strategies are universals. Those of you who are in the Hermean world know perfectly well that we have to be knowledgeable about Hermean norms and strategies. But we don't want them to dominate or to destroy Hestian thinking. Coming back to some of what I've heard here, which is that we can claim our territory, we can move into the world with a positive conviction that not only are we home economists but that Home Economics, fully rounded, committed to women and families, is a kind of feminism in and of itself.

We might even play with the idea that when we speak with other people we are Hestian feminists. Let them deal with that. Let them ask you what a Hestian feminist is. Let them invite you to speak about Hestian feminism. Let them think about the integrative power of a discipline that has in the past, and continues, and in the future will pull together the fragmented world that they are living in. I guess it's a little arrogant, but I do think they need us. I think that with the motivation we have as home economists (our notion of service is so profound and we are so mission oriented in our Hestian feelings), we just have to be patient and tolerant until they are made to see that destroying Home Economics is not pro women. It is pro patriarchy. If feminists are the enemies of hearth and home, perhaps they really can't help it! They are not evolved yet to the point of understanding how limiting for women's lives these Hermean conceptions are. So I'm going to invite you to consider that when you came to this conference you were talking as a home economist, and I hope you're leaving today as a Hestian feminist.

REFLECTIONS

HESTIAN WAYS OF KNOWING

Dialogue belongs to the nature of human beings, as beings of communication. Dialogue seals the act of knowing, which is never individual, even though it has its individual dimensions.

Paolo Freire
A Pedagogy for Liberation.

AS I REVIEWED and edited the Belcourt conference tapes I was more than ever convinced that Home Economics reflects women's ways of being in the world and women's ways of knowing. Those of us who took part in the conference were a varied group, of different ages and ethnic backgrounds. Together we entered a uniquely female mode of knowing in a uniquely Hestian space, Belcourt Centre in South Rustico. Its peaceful, pastoral atmosphere encouraged the participants to leave the stressors of their usual routines behind and look inward for a time. Selves and minds that had been tuned to "other voices" in the "outer world" gradually tuned in to their "inner voices" and to one another. Thoughts and feelings once experienced as separate and personal were shared. Many acknowledged a sense of having been "battered" psychically and emotionally because of their allegiance to Home Economics. They had remained in a field that, over three decades, has been brutally assaulted by both men and feminists who charge Home Economics with failing to keep up with the times and for appearing to be involved with trivial "women's work" or with promoting traditional roles in the household. As women shared experiences, they began to trust themselves and each other. Their sharing transcended their separateness, and the "common threads" of their experience were woven together to form a new pattern that revealed a community of Hestian interest.

Some months after the Belcourt conference, I read *Women's Ways of Knowing* by Mary Field Belenky, Blythe McVicker Clinchy, Nancy Rule

Goldberger, and Jill Mattuck Tarule. Their volume, subtitled *"The Development of Self, Voice, and Mind,"* is based on interviews with women. Analysis of their interviews discloses the epistemological processes women cultivate and value but which prevailing patriarchal disciplines dispute and deprecate. Their work provides a superb interpretive model for reflecting on our meeting at Belcourt. They note:

> *Subjectivism is for women a position from which they redefine the nature of authority. It is the position at which their views of experts and expertise undergo radical change. The orientation to authority shifts from external to internal. (p. 68)*

According to Belenky et al. women's ways of knowing can be traced through several developmental stages, beginning with silently listening to the voice of authority, or *received knowledge*. However, it becomes clear that the prescriptions of received knowledge do not always accord with women's own experience. As women acknowledge the significance of their own first-hand experience, they hear their own "inner voice." In so doing, they find a new source of strength in *subjective knowledge*. This progress from received knowledge to subjective knowledge was evident in the early stage of the Belcourt meetings. As women gained confidence in their subjective knowledge, they realized that their knowledge was not legitimated in a male-dominated knowledge system. I believe that Home Economics is an attempt to legitimate women's gender-intensive (but by no means gender-exclusive) experience and to codify it as a knowledge system. (Thompson, 1984)

Women move from the notion of an impersonal authoritarian truth to an authentic truth that reflects multiple personal truths (p. 66). They take a risk when they experience this mode of knowing. They distrust logic, analysis, abstraction, and even language itself (p. 71). They see these methods as alien territory—a territory I call the Hermean domain. Hermean "authoritative" views devalue home economists' activities and experiences in the Hestian domain and render them invisible. Hestian thinkers are radical—often in a quiet way. They challenge the structures of knowledge imposed on them without their consent—either historically or contemporaneously. Yet Hermean experts ("external" authorities) are listened to. Women still turn to male authorities for advice on child care, marriage, and household work rather than to home economists, who are Hestian experts. Women who value only the modes of the Hermean knowledge system ignore an important aspect of women's ways of knowing. They fail to challenge the premises of Hermean knowledge. Women who find their "place" in the Hermean domain often alienate themselves from those who maintain that there is also a significant "place" for women and men in the Hestian domain. They fail to recognize that knowledge is necessary for this domain as well. We need dependable knowledge for an informed everyday existence.

As women press the boundaries of their knowing, they seek new conceptions of truth. Rules and roles, dictated by Hermean authority, no longer seem so absolute. Relationships are redefined. For those operating in the Hestian mode, the condition of being "in relation" is more significant than the condition of being "in control". Instead of adopting the public, rational, analytic Hermean mode, the women at Belcourt shared, respected, and validated one another's feelings, intuitions, and previously "unvoiced" concerns.

Belenky et al. show that a major challenge for the future is the integration of intuition and reason, of feeling and thinking. They distinguish between two types of *procedural knowledge: separate knowing* and *connected knowing*. They write:

> *Separate knowers speak a public language. They exhibit their knowledge in a series of public performances, and address their messages not to themselves or to intimate friends but to an audience of relative strangers. Often, the primary purpose of their words is not to express personally meaningful ideas but to manipulate the listener's reactions, and they see the listener not as an ally in conversation but as a potentially hostile judge. (p. 108)*

By contrast, there is the mode of connected knowing:

> *Connected knowers develop procedures for gaining access to other people's knowledge. At the heart of these procedures is the capacity for empathy. Since knowledge comes from experience, the only way they can hope to understand another person's ideas is to try to share the experience that has led the person to form the idea. (p. 113)*

I believe that empathy led to shared meaning at Belcourt. Separate knowing is essentially autonomous, i.e. separate from others, while connected knowing is essentially in relationship, i.e. connected to others. The separate self experiences relationships in terms of reciprocity, considering others as it wishes to be considered. It sets itself up as the compass point to which relationships are oriented and by which they are measured. By contrast, the connected self experiences relationships as a response to others in their own terms. Belenky et al. acknowledge that the two types of knowing are not gender-specific, although they may be gender-related with more women than men tipping in one direction than the other. As shared with conference participants my own view is that impersonal thinking, where reason is detached from personality, is a form of separate knowing that I call "Hermean." The type of thinking where personality and reasoning recognize relationships as part of the process of gaining knowledge is a form of connected knowing that I call "Hestian." In Belenky et al.'s view:

> Connected knowers begin with an interest in the facts of other people's lives, but they gradually shift the focus to other people's ways of thinking. As in all procedural knowing, it is the form rather than the content of knowledge that is central. Separate knowers learn through explicit formal instruction. Connected knowers learn through empathy. Both learn to get out from behind their own eyes and use a different lens . . . (p. 115)

As women find their voice through the new feminist scholarship, much that has been invisible in Home Economics will become visible. Many women scholars conform to Hermean norms as a precondition for acceptance in academic life which, by and large, is Hermean. Some men defy convention and adopt Hestian norms. Polarized gender-type thinking perpetuates sex stereotypes, as conference participants recognized when the "stereotype sisters" were discussed. Thinking along a Hestian/Hermean continuum allows for a greater appreciation of human diversity and a genuine respect for pluralism. Belenky et al. also state that connected knowers try to understand texts by imagining themselves into the author's mind (p. 121). This is how a Hestian hermeneutic can provide a new lens of analysis for Home Economics.

Established ways of knowing (which rely on rationalist and impersonal modes of reasoning) are challenged by ways of knowing that seek to integrate thinking and feeling. When women weave together the threads of rational and emotional experience and integrate objective and subjective knowing, they are embarking on a way of knowing described by Belenky et al. as *constructed knowledge* (p. 134). They say:

> To see that all knowledge is a construction and that truth is a matter of the context in which it is embedded is to greatly expand the possibilities of how to think about anything, even those things we consider to be the most elementary and obvious. (p. 138)

Constructed knowledge, as reported by the women at Belcourt and in the sample in the Belenky study, integrates the self, voice, and mind as women are no longer dominated or intimidated by the received wisdom of a patriarchal knowledge system. Women engaged in constructing knowledge show a high tolerance for internal contradiction and ambiguity. Women come to constructed knowledge as they sort out the pieces of the self and find an authentic voice in which to communicate their experience. For me, that voice is Hestian.

The women at Belcourt found their Hestian voice! Home Economics, as a discipline of everyday life; constructs and integrates knowledge for the Hestian domain. I believe that, when the Belcourt conference concluded, the participants had moved from the stage of being respectful recipients of authoritative knowledge to a group that affirmed their subjective knowing. Linked through empathy, they reached the stage of connected knowing. They concluded with an effort at constructing knowledge and integrating that knowledge that they might reflect on it further.

Home Economics is a discipline predicated on connected and integrated knowledge rather than on separate and fragmented knowledge. As experts on evaluating and re-evaluating Hermean knowledge and translating it for everyday use in the Hestian domain, home economists have never abandoned their commitment to the household, home, and family. Home economists, as they experienced their profession at the Belcourt workshop, would fall into the category of "true constructivists" because, as Belenky et al. define it, they revealed an appreciation for complexity and a sense of humility about their knowledge (p. 139). With only a minor change of "home economist" for "constructivist," it becomes possible to recognize home economists as truth-seekers who endeavour to reconcile conflicting ideas into a comprehensive and harmonious system of knowledge essential for experiencing satisfaction in everyday life. Unlike those thinkers who remain separated by the boundaries of the male-defined disciplines, home economists put the knowledge from each discipline into their own service. They are now integrating feminist theory and the new scholarship on women into the knowledge system of Home Economics. Home economists at Belcourt made the connection between theory and practice.

Home economists piece together neglected and rejected scraps of knowledge. They are the mosaic-makers, the weavers, and the quilters of ideas. Their struggle to connect and find new patterns in knowledge is a unique form of order-making in the world. Their sense of Hestian order can better be appreciated as others learn to value connected and integrated knowledge. For other Hestian knowledge seekers, a discipline is waiting to receive them, as it was waiting to receive me.

Patricia J. Thompson
Lehman College
The City University of New York
The Bronx , New York, 10468
May 1987

BIBLIOGRAPHY

The titles listed in the Bibliography are those that relate directly to the Hestian/Hermean conceptualization and the dynamics of the dialogue that evolved over the three-day workshop at Rustico.

Bolen, Jean Shinoda. *Goddesses in Everywoman: A New Psychology of Women.* Foreword by Gloria Steinem. New York: Harper-Colophon, 1984.

Braudel, Fernand. *The Structures of Everyday Life.* Tr. by Sian Reynolds. New York: Harper & Row, 1981.

de Beauvoir, Simone. *The Second Sex.* 1952. Reprint. New York: Vintage Books, 1974.

Gilligan, Carol. *In A Different Voice: Psychological Theory and Women's Development.* Cambridge, MA: Harvard University Press, 1982.

Jung, C.J. *Psychological Types.* Rev. by F.C. Hull of the Tr. by H.G. Baynes. Bollingen Series XX. Princeton, NJ: Princeton University Press, 1971.

Martin, M. Th. Henri. *Memoire Sur La Signification Cosmographique du mythe d'Hestia Dans La Croyance Antique Des Grecs.* Paris: Imprimerie Nationale, 1874.

Newman, Molly and Barbara Damashek. *Quilters.* New York: Dramatists Play Service, Inc., 1986.

Stoianovich, Traian. *French Historical Method: The Annales Paradigm.* Foreword by Fernand Braudel. Ithaca, N.Y.: Cornell University Press, 1976.

Thompson, Patricia J. "Home Economics: A Knowledge System—Not a Gender System." In Patricia J. Thompson, ed. *Knowledge, Technology, and Family Change.* Fourth Yearbook of the Teacher Education Section of the American Home Economics Association. Bloomington, IL: McKnight Publishing Company, 1984, pp. 317–346.

Thompson, Patricia J. "Home Economics and the Hestian Mode." *Illinois Teacher of Home Economics* 29:1 (January/February, 1986), pp. 87–91.

Thompson, Patricia J. "Myth for Modern Home Economics Empowerment—Making Visible Our Hestian World." *What's New in Home Economics* (Mar./Apr.), 1986.

Thompson, Patricia J. "Beyond Gender: Equity Issues for Home Economics Education." *Theory Into Practice* 25:4 (Spring 1986), pp. 276–283.

Thompson, Patricia J. "Hestian Hermeneutics: A Lens of Analysis for Home Economics." In Linda Peterat, ed. *The Conversation and Company of Educated Women: A Colloquy on Home Economics Education.* Special Publication of *Illinois Teacher of Home Economics,* 1986, pp. 11–17, 62–63.

Vandergaag, Nancy (text) and Em Lachance (cartoons) "Step into Spring with the Stereotype Sisters", *Common Ground*, vol. 5, no. 3, July 1986, (insert after p.12).

Vern'ant, Jean Pierre. *Myth and Thought Among the Greeks*. London: Routledge & Kegan Paul, 1982.

Also of interest are the following titles, which came to my attention after the conference:

Paris, Ginette. *Pagan Meditations: Aphrodite, Hestia, Artemis*. Dallas, TX: Spring Publications, 1986.

Porter, J.M., ed. *Sophia and Praxis: The Boundaries of Politics*. Chatham, NJ: Chatham House Publishers, Inc., 1984.

The dynamics of the conference can be examined by comparison with the following work:

Belenky, Mary Field, Blythe McVicker Clinchy, Nancy Ruth Goldberger, and Jill Mattuck Tarule. *Women's Ways of Knowing: The Development of Self, Voice, and Mind*. New York: Basic Books, 1986.

SUBJECT INDEX

106

Jewish, 67
oikos and, 8, 22
private domain and, 8, 18, 24
femininity, 14, 15
feminism,
Hestian, 95
Home Economics as, 95
Liberal, 95
Marxist, 95
Radical, 95
rejection of Home Economics,
92-93, 94
Socialist, 95
feminist movement, 15, 34, 39, 64
feminist theory, Home Economics
and, xi, 7, 11, 24, 39, 94
fire, symbolism of, 10, 25-26, 27
65, 67, 68, 69, 79, 83, 90
flextime, 36
food, as primal necessity, 7, 9
14, 27, 71

gender, 6, 7-8, 14, 21, 22, 39,
48, 64, 99
Home Economics and, 7
language and, 21
goddesses, 62, 64
gossip,
as communication, 58
as stereotype, 58
grandparents, 52

handicapped, 53-56
hearth, symbolism of, 10, 25-26, 64
65
hegemony, Hermean, 83
hemispheres (brain), 11
history,
Hermean, 23-24
Hestian, 23-24, 29-30
Home Economics
as a discipline, 2-3, 4-6, 13, 21,
28, 29, 40, 76, 77, 84
as a Hestian discipline, 14, 40
83, 92, 98, 100
as a knowledge system, 98
as an integrative (interdisciplinary) discipline, 28, 70, 74, 81,
89-91, 95, 101

as an intellectual challenge, 4
as a "women's field," 76, 99
as Hestian history, 24, 29
as holistic education, 78-79
homemaking, as Hestian vocation,
74
household, 17, 22, 66, 101
as spatial domain, 8, 22, 27, 65
66, 68, 81
oikos and, 8
housekeeping, as Hestian labor,
64, 68
housework, as Hestian labor, 64,
98,
hunger, children and, 82

intuition, 74, 99
invisibility,
everyday activities, and, 8
Home Economics and, 6, 11, 91,
93, 98
women and, 6-7,

knowledge,
authoritarian, 98-100
connected, 99-101
constructed, 100-101
Hermean perspective on, 12, 24
70-71, 99
Hestian perspective on, 29-30,
48, 70-71, 98-99
procedural, 99
received, 98
structure of, 98
subjective, 98

labor, Hestian, 64, 74
language, 38-39, 92
feminist theory and, 37
Hermean, 17, 22, 71
Hestian, 17, 22, 27, 28, 38, 90
women and, 12, 17, 37-38
life, everyday, 9, 21, 27, 28-29, 52
64, 69, 70, 77, 78, 88, 90, 95
life, private, 7
life, public, 7

management (household/home),
17, 22, 25, 29, 64, 72, 80-81, 88,
(see also oikonomeia)

NAME INDEX